Let's W
The Yorkshire Coast

Let's Walk
The Yorkshire Coast

Stephen I. Robinson

BARLEY • PUBLISHING
2019

First published 2019

Barley Publishing
10 Mill Green View
Swarcliffe
Leeds LS14 5JT

www.hm-walks.co.uk

ISBN 978-1-898550-15-0

Printed in Great Britain by:
Charlesworth Press
Flanshaw Way, Flanshaw Lane
Wakefeld, WF2 9LP
Telephone: 01924 204 830

The Caedmon Cross, Whitby

'Nobody, who approaches Whitby Abbey in the true spirit of pilgrimage, can look on that broken church on the cliff-top without being moved. In certain lights, especially at twilight and dawn, it takes on an ethereal beauty that I have not seen elsewhere.'

Alfred J. Brown,
Tramping in Yorkshire – North and East, (1932).

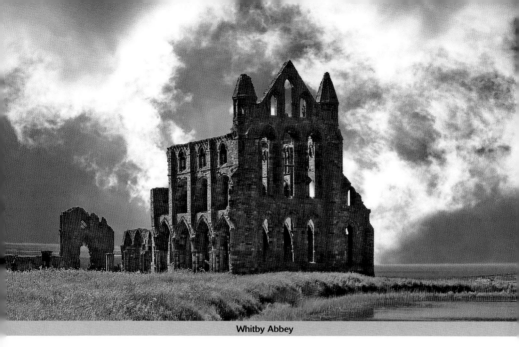

Whitby Abbey

Contents

Acknowledgements

The preparation of this guide would not have been possible without the advice and encouragement of so many lovely, and helpful people. To all those who provided me with information, my gratitude is boundless, and I hope the finished product meets with their approval.

In particular, I would like to express my sincere thanks to David and June Thornton for their editorial advice, proofreading, valuable suggestions and also for correcting my errors. Special thanks to Stephen Spellman, who accompanied me on many of the walks, for the cover design and his assistance with the inside layout and selection of photographs. I would also like to extend my thanks to the North York Moors National Park for checking the accuracy of the mapping and route directions within the National Park.

I would also like to express my gratitude to the following individuals and organisations for giving me permission to use their photographs: Theadora Crocker, Gordon Bell, Bob Cockshott, Shutterstock.com, badobadop.co.uk, Tees Archaeology, Whitby Museum and Jill Tate/Landmark Trust. The copyright for each these photographs is also acknowledged in the list of illustrations.

Finally, I would like to thank everyone who replied to my letters and emails regarding the various areas and subjects covered in the book.

Disclaimer

While all reasonable efforts have been made to ensure that the details contained within this guide were correct at the time of publication, neither the author nor the publisher can accept any responsibility for errors or omissions, or for changes in the information provided. The author has walked and researched the entire route for the compilation of this guide. However, neither the author nor the publisher can accept any responsibility in connection with any trespass arising from the use of the promoted route or any associated route.

It is the responsibility of all individuals undertaking outdoor pursuits to approach the activity with caution, and if inexperienced, they should do so under appropriate supervision. They should also carry the relevant maps and equipment, wear appropriate clothing and suitable footwear. The pastime described in this book is strenuous, and individuals should ensure that they are suitably fit before attempting to undertake it.

Heritage Coast stone marker

List of Illustrations

All maps and photographs © S. I. Robinson unless credited otherwise above.

Approaching the coast from Warsett Hill, near Saltburn

Robin Hood's Bay from Ravenscar

Introduction

Yorkshire's dramatic coastline embraces some of the UK's most beautiful and unspoilt countryside, comprising picturesque fishing villages, rocky cliffs, wooded valleys and sheltered bays with golden sandy beaches – offering a memorable experience for visitors.

The Yorkshire Coast is an internationally famous stretch of coastline, running between the Tees estuary and the Humber estuary. Historically, the coastal region connecting these two estuaries incorporated the East and North Ridings of Yorkshire. However, in 1974 the Boundary Commission changed the borders, and the coastline now comprises Redcar and Cleveland, North Yorkshire and the East Riding of Yorkshire.

Moreover, the Yorkshire coastline is home to three of over forty nationally designated Heritage Coasts in England and Wales. This designation provides special protection to delicate areas of the coast, ensuring that they remain unexploited by industry and tourism. Two of these, Spurn Point and the

Flamborough Headland, are in the East Riding. The third and most extended section is the North Yorkshire and Cleveland Heritage Coast, which lies between Saltburn and Scalby Mills near Scarborough, a distance of 36 miles (58km). The latter incorporates the area explored by the walks in this book, and its entire length is accessible via the Cleveland Way National Trail.

The Cleveland Way covers a distance of 109 miles (175km) sweeping around the edge of the North York Moors National Park to Saltburn, before heading south along the Heritage Coast to Filey Brigg. The coastal section of the trail also constitutes part of the England Coast Path, which will eventually follow the entire coastline of England. When completed, it will be the world's longest coastal path, covering a distance of around 2795 miles (4498km). Furthermore, the Heritage Coast forms part of the North Sea Trail, which aims to provide a trail around the coastlines of all the countries that border the North Sea. The route will pass through Scotland, England,

Netherlands, Germany, Denmark, Sweden and Norway, comprising a total distance of approximately 3107 miles (5000km).

Popularly known as the Dinosaur Coast, this dramatic coastline is world famous for its geological exposures and rich fossil resources. Due to the instability of the sea cliffs, the shoreline continually changes and just about everywhere along the coast from Saltburn to Scarborough fossils are prolific in the exposed rocks. These rocks, formed during the Jurassic period between 200 and 145 million years ago, contain the fossilised remains of the plants and animals from that era and dinosaur footprints!

The most common fossils found hereabouts are ammonites, sometimes called snakestones owing to their likeness to coiled serpents. According to a local legend, ammonites originated when the Abbess Hilda of Whitby, later St Hilda, drove a plague of snakes over the cliff at Whitby and one species of ammonite, named Hildoceras,

Captain Cook's Statue, Whitby

honours this mythical act. Furthermore, there are footprints of three-toed carnivorous theropods and plant-eating sauropods which once roamed the mudflats in search of food. In 2015 part of the vertebra belonging to a sauropod fell out of a cliff face near Whitby. Experts have since identified this as Britain's oldest sauropod dinosaur, dating back about 176 million years. The sauropods had distinctive long necks and tails with small heads and large bodies. Some species grew up to 115 feet (35m) long, possibly weighing up to 80 tonnes. They were the largest land animals that have ever lived on Earth.

To confront the dinosaurs more personally, visit the Rotunda Museum, the home of 'Scarborough's Lost Dinosaurs'. The exhibits include fossilised evidence of dinosaurs, which roamed around the neighbourhood during the Jurassic period. The Rotunda, which opened in 1829, is one of the world's first purpose-built museums, designed by William 'Strata' Smith, known as the father of English geology. The museum has many other fascinating items, including; the Gristhorpe Man – the well-preserved skeleton and log coffin of a Bronze Age warrior, which is an excellent example of a tree burial in Britain.

The Yorkshire Coast also possesses many sites of archaeological and historical interest, testifying to mankind's impact on the landscape. Between the seventeenth and nineteenth centuries, mining and quarrying removed vast quantities of alum, ironstone and jet from the coastal cliffs. When the railways reached the area, it became much more accessible and allowed large-scale mining to begin. In turn, this led to the industrial expansion of Middlesbrough and established the Teesside iron and steel industry. Although nature has helped to reduce the scars left behind by this exploitation, there are still many relics from that era to interest industrial archaeologists.

In the fourth century AD, the Romans constructed a series of watchtowers on the high ground between the Humber and Tees estuaries. One of their primary functions was

A heavy 'roak' creeping inland near Skinningrove

to warn against the threat of Anglo-Saxon raids; the towers signalled to land-based patrols to give them time to prepare for the seaborne attacks. During World War II, the construction of reinforced concrete pillboxes, anti-tank cubes and radar installations helped to secure the coastline against the threat of an expected Nazi invasion. Some features of this period remain on the shoreline and clifftops.

Between 1700 and 1850 many of the picturesque fishing villages like Staithes and Robin Hood's Bay were notorious as smuggling ports. Captain Cook, the British navigator and explorer, began his seafaring career at Whitby, and Whitby Abbey provided the setting for Bram Stoker's novel, *Dracula*. During the Civil War, Scarborough Castle endured two sieges, and in the opening months of World War I, German battleships shelled the town and castle from the bay. These events undoubtedly confirm that the Yorkshire Coast has endured a turbulent and intriguing history.

One of the eeriest phenomena along the Yorkshire Coast is the 'roak' – a damp sea fog which creeps inland from the North Sea, and hugs the high ground across the moors. The Yorkshire roaks are infamous, with visibility reduced to a few yards, the air becomes heavy with chilling dampness. In folk stories, 'roaks are the cause of souls lost, sometimes forever, in the moorland wilderness.'

Yorkshire's coastline is a fantastic place for marine life with some of Europe's most fertile fishing seas. Beneath the waves, there are lobsters, octopus, sea squirts, mussels and more than 100 species of seaweed including kelp forests. In late summer and autumn, vast shoals of mackerel and herring migrate to the shallower, inshore waters to spawn. They are closely pursued by whales, dolphins, sharks, seals and flocks of seabirds in search of food. The coastal cliffs provide vital nesting sites for seabird colonies, including cormorants, gannets, guillemots, herring gulls, kittiwakes and puffins.

The wealth and variety of these natural and man-made attributes have created a unique contrast of landscapes – a prize for everyone to savour and enjoy. However, the coastline is susceptible to landslips which may result in the trail being diverted. If you should encounter a diversion, ALWAYS follow the signs – NEVER 'carry on regardless!'

Key to the Maps

Route	Cairn/Hilltop
Other Paths	OS Column
Detours	Buildings
Permitted Paths	Boundary Stone
Rivers/Streams	Viewpoint
Crags/Scars	Car Park
Villages/Towns	Bus Route
Woodland	Camping
A Road	Caravans
B Road	Pub
Minor Road	Cafe/Refreshments
Unnamed Road	Toilets
Unfenced Road	Telephone
Farm Road/Cart Track	Accommodation
Railway ● Station	Tourist Information
Sand, Shingle	Youth Hostel
Rocks	10 Miles covered
Cliffs	① Starting point of each map
North Sea	② Intermediate points
Mean High Water	Ⓐ Detours and alternative routes
National Park Boundary	Route direction arrows

14

About the Walks

The walks described in this guide explore the stunning coastal scenery of the North Yorkshire and Cleveland Heritage Coast. They also provide an opportunity to visit some of the beautiful villages and attractions further inland.

All the walks follow circular routes ranging from 6 to 8¾ miles (9.65 to 14.08km). Each walk starts at a car park where one is available, or at a place where it is possible to park safely without obstructing gateways or causing inconvenience to others.

Each map has the route marked in red with numbered arrow pointers for each section of the walk, the colours indicate:

① The suggested starting point of the walk.

② The intermediate points on each map.

Ⓐ Detours and alternative paths.

The pointers relate to the detailed directions, which also include a grid reference for the starting point of each stage. When used together these features should help to avoid confusion, although common sense and some preliminary map reading experience are always advantageous. This simplified format should enable most people to follow the route with ease.

Final surveys of the walks took place between January and March 2019. However, from time to time walls, fences and hedges may be removed, stiles and gates re-sited, new forestry established and buildings demolished. Therefore, it is advisable to take the relevant Ordnance Survey maps and a compass with you. These will help to determine landmarks and locate alternative routes where necessary. All the walks described in this guide require just one OS map: Explorer OL27 (1:25,000) *North York Moors, Eastern Area.*

The time given for the completion of each walk is approximate and does not include any allowance for lunch breaks, photo stops or sightseeing. As a rule of thumb, adding one-third of the stated time for stops should be sufficient. When accompanied by young children, extra walking time will have to be allowed. Furthermore, extended stays at any of the inns or tea shops en route will also have to be added to the time.

Sometimes it may become necessary to divert paths to carry out maintenance work, or because the route has changed. This is particularly relevant along the Cleveland Way National Trail, which is continually under threat from landslips caused by coastal erosion. Should this occur, always follow the diversion signs along the path and do not attempt to continue along the promoted routes of this guide.

The Countryside Code

Respect Protect Enjoy

Respect other people
• Consider the local community and other people enjoying the outdoors
• Leave gates and property as you find them and follow paths unless wider access is available

Protect the natural environment
• Leave no trace of your visit and take your litter home
• Keep dogs under effective control

Enjoy the outdoors
• Plan ahead and be prepared
• Follow advice and local signs

Warsett Hill and Saltburn Gill

FROM SALTBURN – 8 MILES (12.9KM)

Railway line along Hunt Cliff

This exhilarating walk from Saltburn-by-the-Sea has many impressive features including a charm bracelet, a clifftop railway and a nature reserve. The coastal scenery is invigorating with beautiful sandy beaches and towering cliffs.

The majority of Saltburn's charms as a Victorian seaside resort extend their appeal to the visitors of today, including the colourful Italian Gardens, a miniature railway and its enticing golden sands. The town also boasts one of the world's oldest water balanced inclined tramways which opened in 1884. The tramway links the town to its resplendent pleasure pier; the last surviving iron pier on England's north-east coastline. When it opened in May 1869, Saltburn Pier was 1500 feet (457m) long and had a landing stage for paddle-steamers. However, storm damage has taken its toll over the years and the pier's length today is just 681 feet (208m). (See *Miscellanea* page 62 for further information).

From Saltburn, our route ascends onto Hunt Cliff and follows a clifftop path along the Cleveland Way. The high cliffs hereabouts support substantial colonies of seabirds, particularly cormorants, fulmars, herring gulls and kittiwakes. The kittiwake lives out at sea feeding on small fish, shrimps and squid, and only comes ashore to breed; its loud, repetitive 'kitti-waak' call is unmistakable.

Further along the cliff, an information point records that a Roman signal station existed near here. Excavations in 1911-12 unearthed coins dating from AD 362-392 as well as brooches, sandals, wooden bowls, pottery and a jet finger ring. The Hunt Cliff signal station was one of five such watchtowers sited along the Yorkshire coast between the Humber and Tyne estuaries to give early warning of attacks by Anglo-Saxon raiders. Moreover, the turret at Hunt Cliff was 50 feet (15.2m) in length, and the walls were 7½ feet (2.3m) thick, indicating that these defences also served as fortifications. Unfortunately, due to coastal erosion, all traces of the site have since disappeared.

The railway line running along the edge of Hunt Cliff is the remains of the former Whitby, Redcar and Middlesbrough Union Railway.

The track followed a very scenic coastal route and was open to passenger traffic between 1875 and 1958, linking communities along the East Coast. However, these days the railway serves the sole purpose of transporting goods and materials to and from the Boulby Potash Mine near Staithes.

Beside the railway line, there are three metal sculptures, produced from steel rolled at Skinningrove. First, the Trawl Door which represents the local fishing industry. Trawl doors are plates used to keep nets open while trawling for fish. Next, the Pillar, with four shapes attached, symbolising earth, air, sky and water. Finally, the Hunt Cliff Circle, which resembles a charm bracelet with ten charms suspended from the top. Each charm represents a story of local culture, tradition or folklore. The buildings across the railway line are the remains of the Guibal Fanhouse, which provided vital ventilation to the Hunt Cliff Ironstone Mine.

Leaving the sculptures behind we descend along Cattersty Cliff, returning to sea level at Cattersty Sands, which has a spectacular long beach with clear water, beautiful sands and rocks at either end. The route passes the old jetty to reach Skinningrove.

During the early nineteenth century, Skinningrove was a small fishing hamlet. However, in 1847 after the discovery of ironstone seams in the valley, the village undertook a dramatic transformation. Cleveland's first ironstone mine opened at Skinningrove in 1848; it was one of eighty-three ironstone mines in the region. In 1874 iron smelting began nearby and the village expanded rapidly to satisfy the demand for iron. The smelting works supplied the metal for building bridges and railways across Europe, America, Africa, India and Australia. More recently, Skinningrove provided 3500 tonnes of special steel profiles for the aircraft carrier HMS *Queen Elizabeth*, which is the largest warship ever built for the Royal Navy.

After exploring the village, we return to Hunt Cliff and ascend onto Warsett Hill. From the summit, there are magnificent views across Saltburn towards Teesmouth, and on a bright day Roseberry Topping is visible to the south-west. The route continues into Brotton, where we are welcomed by some impressive badger sculptures carved by Steve Iredale – a talented chainsaw sculptor from Staithes. Incidentally, Brotton was the birthplace of Charles Robinson Sykes 1875-1950. He designed *the Spirit of Ecstasy*, the bonnet ornament used on Rolls-Royce cars since 1909.

After a brief road walk, we follow a path to the Saltburn Gill Nature Reserve. The reserve is a wildlife-rich woodland with a dense canopy of oak and ash trees. The forest has remained relatively undisturbed since the 1600s and is representative of the ancient forests which once covered East Cleveland.

In spring, the yellow flowers of lesser celandine bathe the woodland floor with colour, followed by carpets of bluebells, violets and the pungent aroma of wild garlic fills the air. The reserve supports resident birds such as the robin, blackbird and wren; and summer sees the arrival of the migrants starting with the chiffchaff, followed by willow warbler, blackcap and spotted flycatcher. With a little luck and patience, roe deer sightings are a possibility. Whatever the season, even after the autumn leaves have fallen from the trees, Saltburn Gill is always worthy of a visit.

Just a few minutes after leaving the reserve we arrive back at the seafront – and perhaps some refreshments are in order!

Badger sculptures, Brotton

17

Start/Parking: Cat Nab car park, Saltburn Bank, Saltburn-by-the-Sea TS12 1NY.

Location: Saltburn-by-the-Sea is situated on the North Sea coastline, off the A174 Thornaby-on-Tees to Whitby road 6 miles (9.5km) south-east of Redcar.

Grid Ref: NZ 668 215. – **Postcode:** Cat Nab car park, TS12 1NY.

Distance: 8 miles (12.9km) circular. Allow 4½ hrs walking time.

Total Ascent: 1727 feet (526m). – **Maximum Elevation:** 545 feet (166m).

OS Maps: Explorer OL27 (1:25,000) *North York Moors, Eastern Area* or Landranger 94 (1:50,000) *Whitby and Esk Dale*.

Refreshments: Skinningrove, Brotton and Saltburn.

Public Toilets: Saltburn – Cat Nab car park; Skinningrove – near the road bridge.

Other: Bus service, telephone, Cleveland Ironstone Mining Museum.

Alternative Start: Skinningrove Jetty, Marine Terrace TS13 4BJ. Use directions from point 9.

1 **668215** Leave the car park turn right and follow the road along the seafront, passing to the right of the Ship Inn.

2 **670215** Leave the road via a track on left *(SP Cleveland Way - Skinningrove 3.5m)*. Ascend a stepped path to the clifftop.

3 **672215** Continue along the edge of Hunt Cliff, passing the site of a Roman signal station.

4 **688218** Go through the gate and head towards the railway track. Follow a clear path beside the line, passing some steel sculptures.

5 **696216** Bear left and descend to the left of an enclosure *(NT Warsett Hill)*. Continue along the clifftop passing point 10 **(A)**.

A **699213** To shorten the route by about 2½ miles (4km). Cross the wooden step stile on the right and head across the field to the railway line. Now follow instructions from point 11.

6 **701211** Turn right and follow an enclosed path for a short distance. Turn left through a gap in the hedge and return to the clifftop. Begin a gradual descent along Cattersty Cliff to a signpost.

7 **706205** Turn left *(SP Cleveland Way)* and descend a stepped path towards the beach, and then follow a sandy path to the old jetty.

8 **711204** Go through a gap in the jetty, bear right and follow a broad track leading to the car park at Skinningrove.

9 **713201** After exploring the village, retrace the outward route passing points 8, 7 and 6 to reach point 10 **(A)**.

10 **699213** Cross the wooden step stile on the left and head across the field to the railway line.

11 **698212** Continue via two step stiles, crossing the railway line, **DANGER: STOP, LOOK, LISTEN before crossing the railway line!** Head directly across the field and cross a step stile. Continue in the same direction across the next field.

12 **694214** Halfway across the field, the right of way joins another track sweeping around to the right. Continue through two open gateways and a step stile to reach the railway line again.

B **694214** Warsett Hill is open access land, therefore you may continue to the summit *(recommended route)*. At the OS column, turn left, cross a step stile and descend along the right boundary, turn left and continue over a wooden step stile. Now follow instructions from point 13.

13 **688215** Cross the railway line via two step stiles. **DANGER: STOP, LOOK, LISTEN before crossing the railway line!** Follow the left fence through a gate and continue to Brough House Farm.

14 **682215** Turn left at Brough Cottage and follow an enclosed farm lane behind Brough House Farm *(SP Brotton)*. Continue on the farm lane passed Shepherd's House.

15 **685206** Cross the railway via a level crossing. **DANGER: STOP, LOOK, LISTEN before crossing the railway line!** Continue into Brotton, turn right and follow the road under the railway bridge. Continue along the road to Barns Farm opposite the Cedar Nurseries. **CAUTION: Busy road.**

16 **680206** Turn left, *(SP Saltburn Gill)*. Continue on an enclosed farm lane to Barns Farm. Pass to the left of the entrance gates and follow a narrow path through the wood.

17 **678205** Turn right and continue along the boundary of the wood. Go through a gap in the hedge and descend into Saltburn Gill.

18 **674206** Just before reaching the beck, turn right and follow the footpath downstream over walkways and bridges returning to the main road.

19 **669214** The route emerges near the Cat Nab Car Park and the miniature railway.

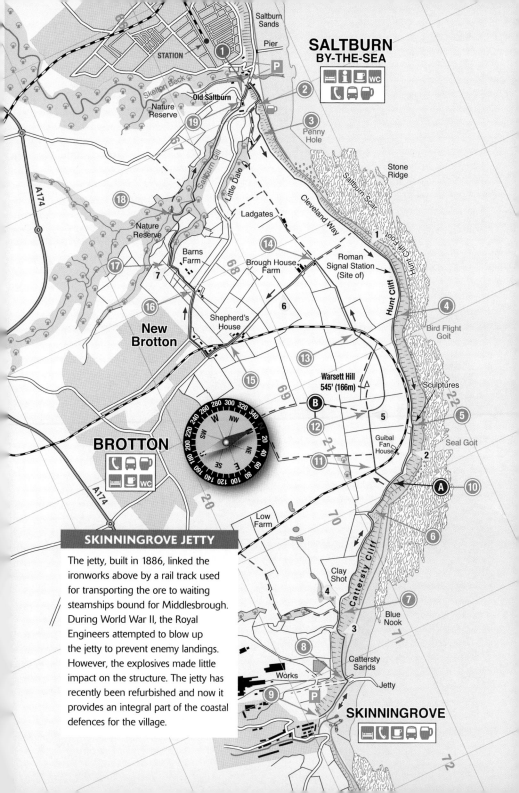

SALTBURN BY-THE-SEA

SKINNINGROVE JETTY

The jetty, built in 1886, linked the ironworks above by a rail track used for transporting the ore to waiting steamships bound for Middlesbrough. During World War II, the Royal Engineers attempted to blow up the jetty to prevent enemy landings. However, the explosives made little impact on the structure. The jetty has recently been refurbished and now it provides an integral part of the coastal defences for the village.

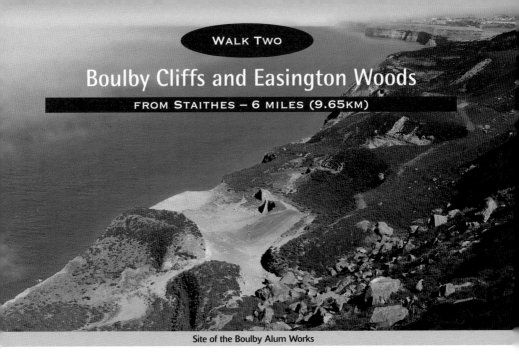

WALK TWO

Boulby Cliffs and Easington Woods

FROM STAITHES — 6 MILES (9.65KM)

Site of the Boulby Alum Works

Starting from the picturesque village of Staithes, this walk ascends from sea level to the highest cliffs on the east coast of England. Along the way, there are remnants of the former alum and ironstone industries and a 'sound mirror' from World War I.

Staithes, pronounced as 'Steers' by the locals, derives its name from 'staithe' which means 'a landing place'. The village was formerly one of the largest fishing ports on the north-east coast. In the early 1900s, eighty full-time fishing boats operated from here. The port still has some part-time fishermen, and it maintains a small fleet of traditional cobles. The distinctive shape of a coble is flat-bottomed with a high bow, and it possibly originates from a Viking design. Boats with flat bottoms were able to launch from and land onto shallow, sandy beaches. Moreover, fishing vessels required high bows to sail on the hazardous North Sea, especially when launching into the surf.

The cliffs of Cowbar Nab standing across Staithes Beck are under the protection of the National Trust. In spring noisy colonies of

kittiwakes, fulmars and the occasional razorbill hustle and bustle for the best nesting sites on the perilous-rocky ledges. The grassy areas near the top provide an essential breeding ground for herring gulls, which add their discord to the melody. Unfortunately, access to Cowbar Nab was not possible at the time of writing. Following a landslip in March 2016, the slopes remain unstable, and it is inadvisable to make any attempt to reach the site until further notice.

The beck is also the local government boundary and the route passes from North Yorkshire into the borough of Redcar and Cleveland as we leave Staithes. After climbing the steep hill from Cowbar, we follow the Cleveland Way to the tiny hamlet of Boulby. The name descends from the old Norse 'Bollebi' which means 'Bolli's Farm' suggesting that it started out as a Viking settlement.

From Boulby, the path climbs steadily to the Boulby Cliffs, the highest sea-cliffs on the east coast of England rising to 666 feet (203m) at Rock Cliff. There is an old tradition that this was the burial site of Beowulf, the sixth-century Scandinavian hero. This legend, based on the epic poem *Beowulf*, was one of the oral tales retold by Anglo-Saxon storytellers to entertain crowds of people on long evenings. Although the original setting of the myth is Scandinavia, some historians and scholars relish giving the story an English slant. According to this version, Beowulf died after slaying a dragon and his people, the Geats, carried his body to a high cliff for cremation on a funeral pyre. Afterwards, they built a burial mound on the high ground overlooking the sea, which they filled with treasure.

The first written record of *Beowulf* dates to around AD 975-1010, making it the oldest surviving manuscript of the longest epic poem in Old English. The local scribes most likely knew of the recently excavated Street House Anglo-Saxon cemetery, dating from the late seventh century, and a Bronze Age round barrow, which both lie nearby. Add in the high Boulby Cliffs to the mixture, and the legend is born!

The coastal scenery is exhilarating, but the landscape below is much more austere and bears the marks of the quarries left behind by the alum and ironstone industries. The alum works at Boulby were one of the most prolific in the area, and operated from the 1650s until their closure in 1871.

Leaving the cliffs behind our route heads inland, passing the OS column to reach the Boulby transmitter mast. An optional detour along the road to the east leads to the Boulby Sound Mirror, a relic of the First World War and a Grade II listed National Monument.

In 1915 Zeppelins began bombing the steelworks at Skinningrove, which was a key factory manufacturing high explosives. These attacks were difficult to defend against. By the time Zeppelins became visible, it was too late to launch any defence. Consequently, the Royal Flying Corps could only destroy the enemy airships after they had delivered their deadly cargo. However, after the placement of 'sound mirrors' at strategic positions along the coast the RFC received early warning of the incoming enemy aircraft, giving

them time to respond more effectively. The Boulby Sound Mirror is a U-shaped concrete structure comprising a thick wall with an inclined face and a concave dish cut into its centre. The mirror worked by reflecting the noise of aircraft engines onto a microphone, which amplified the sound and transmitted it to the headphones of the operator who sat in a trench at the front. These listening posts became obsolete with the invention of radar.

During the descent from Twizzlegill Farm, the grey industrial buildings of the Boulby Potash Mine dominate the panorama with the North Sea as a backdrop. The mine, which opened in 1973, produces around fifty-five per cent of the UK's potash and at 4600 feet (1400m) deep, is the second deepest mine of any kind in Europe. Evidently the mine has a network of underground roads which extend under the North Sea and cover a total distance of 620 miles (1000km). Because of its depth Boulby is a special place for science - 'a quiet place in the Universe' - free of background radiation, one of the projects includes the search for 'Dark Matter'.

After passing through Easington Wood, we reach the site of the Grinkle Park ironstone mine, which began production as a drift mine in 1875. To create sufficient space for mining, Easington Beck was diverted through a culvert, and the valley backfilled with spoil. Although most of the mine workings were destroyed during the construction of the Boulby Potash Mine, remnants of the former furnace house survive and are undergoing conservation. Some of the other remains include a concrete hopper used for loading waste shale onto an aerial cableway for tipping on the coast. Further on we pass the northern portal of the Ridge Lane tramway tunnel, which is 400 yards (365m) in length. Due to the low headroom of the tunnel, the locomotives used for carrying materials and workmen to the mine had open cabs.

The return to Staithes passes through the picturesque hamlet of Dalehouse where a traditional inn, the Fox and Hounds, provides excellent fayre to travellers.

Start/Parking:	Large car park off Staithes Lane, Staithes, TS13 5AD.
Location:	Staithes is situated on the North Sea coastline, off the A174 Thornaby-on-Tees to Whitby road 10½ miles (16.9km) north-west of Whitby.
Grid Ref:	NZ 781 185. – **Postcode:** Staithes Lane, Staithes, TS13 5AD.
Distance:	6 miles (9.65km) circular. Allow 3½ hrs walking time.
Total Ascent:	1073 feet (327m). – **Maximum Elevation:** 689 feet (213m).
OS Maps:	Explorer OL27 (1:25,000) *North York Moors, Eastern Area* or Landranger 94 (1:50,000) *Whitby and Esk Dale.*
Refreshments:	Staithes, Easington and Dalehouse.
Public Toilets:	Staithes, none en route.
Other:	Bus service, telephone, Post Office, gift shops, cafes, fish shop, Captain Cook and Staithes Heritage Centre.

1 **781185** Leave the car park turn right and follow the road into the village, descending steeply to Cleveland Corner *(shop)*.

A **782189** To explore the lower part of the village, turn right here and follow the road to the harbour. Return to this point afterwards and follow the directions given in **point 2.**

2 **782189** Turn left into a narrow alley *(sign Lifeboat Station and Gift Shop)* descend to cross the bridge over Staithes Beck. Turn left and ascend steeply along the road to Cowbar.

3 **779188** Turn right *(SP Cleveland Way)* and follow the lane to a signpost.

4 **770187** Turn right and head towards the clifftop, after a few yards, turn left *(SP Cleveland Way - Skinningrove 4m)*. Cross a large field and then follow an enclosed track returning to the road at Boulby.

5 **763189** Follow the road uphill *(SP Cleveland Way)*. At a junction continue straight ahead, ascending along the cliff. Pass through a kissing gate and continue along the left boundary fence. Follow the path steeply uphill to Rock Cliff.

6 **750196** Leave the clifftop via the wooden step stile on the left and follow an enclosed path over the summit to the Boulby Transmitter Mast.

7 **749192** Turn left and follow the road for a few yards. Leave the road via a gate on the right *(Waymark)*. Continue on a fenced path and then follow the left boundary through two fields.

B **749192** The Boulby Sound Mirror is situated about 550 yards (500m) along the road to the left. However, the mirror is on private land and can only be viewed from the roadside. This is an optional detour and would add about ¾ mile (1km) to the walk.

8 **749186** Go through a gate and then head directly across the field. Pass through another gate and descend along the left boundary hedge. Go through a gate leading to the A174 main road.

9 **749181** Turn right and follow the road for about 30 yards (27m). **CAUTION: Busy road.** Cross the road and continue down the farm lane opposite *(SP Public Footpath)*. At the farm turn left and go through two gates, turn right and continue behind the farm buildings.

10 **751178** At the corner of the field turn left and follow a broad track passing over the summit of the field. Continue across the next field descending gradually to the hedge and the railway line.

11 **757177** Pass through a gap in the hedge and go through a gate. **DANGER: STOP, LOOK, LISTEN before crossing the railway line!** Continue over the line and go through a gate into Easington Woods. Follow a clear path through the wood, turn left onto a broad forest track and follow it to the Grinkle Ironstone Mine furnace house.

12 **762177** The furnace house is situated to the left of the track. From the furnace house, return to the track and follow it to a junction of paths.

13 **764178** Turn right, cross Easington Beck and pass the northern entrance to the former Ridge Lane tramway tunnel.

14 **765179** After about 250 yards (230m) the right of way leaves the track via some steps on the right *(Waymark)*, follow a clear trail ascending through the forest and rejoin the forest track further on. Turn right and continue to the minor road.

15 **770179** Turn left and follow the road to the junction at Dalehouse.

16 **776179** At the junction turn left and follow the road through the hamlet, ascending steeply to the A174 main road. **CAUTION: Busy road.** Turn right and continue ascending to the road junction near the traffic lights.

17 **780181** Turn left at the junction *(SP Staithes ½),* follow the road into the village and return to the car park.

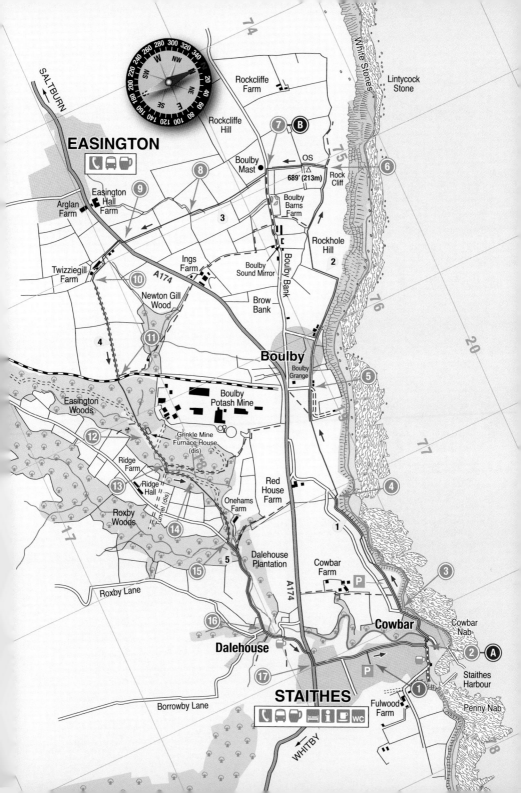

Staithes and Port Mulgrave

FROM RUNSWICK BAY – 7 MILES (11.26KM)

Staithes harbour and Cowbar Nab

There are many dramatic headlands and enchanting bays along Yorkshire's rugged coastline, and this uplifting walk links two of the most attractive coastal villages found along its shores.

Before leaving Runswick Bay, take a few moments to appreciate the spectacular views. The entire length of Runswick Bay's broad sandy beach stretches out below, and in the distance the headland of Kettleness beckons. In the lower part of the village, which we explore more intimately during Walk 4, clusters of gleaming, red-roofed cottages huddle together on the steep hillside, linked by an enticing maze of narrow pedestrian alleyways.

From the car park, we follow the road into Hinderwell, which apparently takes its name from 'Hild's well', a holy well in the grounds of St Hilda's Church. According to legend, while returning to her monastery at Whitby, the Abbess Hilda stopped here, and after praying for water a spring appeared. Subsequently, St Hilda's Well became a pilgrimage site for monks travelling between

the religious houses of Kirkham and Whitby. By tradition, the local children visited St Hilda's Well on Ascension Day. After placing pieces of liquorice into bottles, they filled them with water from the well. The liquorice permeated the water, adding a taste to create a children's drink called Spanish. This event, known as Spanish Water Day, took place at many of the holy wells throughout England.

Another legend associated with St Hilda tells of a plague of snakes, which she turned into stone after driving them over the cliffs at Whitby. Perhaps this explains the presence of the many ammonite fossils found along the coastline, which because of their likeness to coiled serpents, are also known as snakestones. Furthermore, one species of ammonite, named Hildoceras by Victorian geologists, venerates this mythical act.

To leave the village, we pass around a delightful crescent lined with well-kept cottages and join a farm lane, which leads down into the sylvan valley of The Dales. The route continues through the Oakridge Nature Reserve to Dalehouse.

Just across the bridge stands Dalehouse Farm, which earned recognition for breeding and showing Cleveland Bay Horses, England's oldest breed of horse. In the 1960s Her Majesty the Queen purchased a pure-bred Cleveland Bay colt named Mulgrave Supreme from Dalehouse. Moreover, Her Majesty made the horse available at public stud, where Mulgrave Supreme sired many successful offspring, helping to restore popularity in the breed, thus ensuring its future.

After a short ascent to the main road, we reach the picturesque village of Staithes. In addition to fishing, Staithes is also famous for its association with Captain James Cook; here, he discovered his passion for a life at sea. In 1744 James Cook arrived in Staithes to begin his apprenticeship in the shop of William Sanderson. But It was not long before 16-year old James became fascinated by seafaring tales and dreamed of becoming a seaman, and Sanderson realised that the youngster's heart was not in shopkeeping. In July 1746 he found Cook an apprenticeship in the merchant navy with Whitby shipowner Captain John Walker, thus starting his incredible maritime career.

In the High Street, a memorial clock and barometer commemorate the bravery of a local man. George Hanson, a fisherman and head launcher of the Runswick lifeboat, plunged into the sea fully clothed to rescue swimmers in the harbour. After saving a schoolboy, George attempted to rescue another man, tragically both men succumbed to the fury of the waves. The inscription reads 'Erected to honour the memory of George Hanson, a Staithes fisherman who lost his life in a gallant attempt to rescue a drowning bather in a rough sea on Wednesday 28 August 1957.'

Staithes harbour, nestling between the headlands of Cowbar Nab and Penny Nab, has two long breakwaters to reduce the force of the waves and provide much-needed protection to the village. The Cod and Lobster Inn on the quayside has resisted the wrath of the North Sea for centuries, despite being destroyed by fierce storms and rebuilt on at least three occasions. Hopefully, the improved sea defences should prevent that from happening again.

Further exploration of the village reveals an intriguing network of alleys and ginnels, which bear curious names such as Gun Gutter, Slip Top and Dog Loup. The latter is the narrowest street in the UK, and at a mere 18 inches (457mm) in width, stouter walkers may have to shed a few pounds to pass through it!

Leaving Staithes, we follow the Cleveland Way along the clifftop to Port Mulgrave. The track formerly led away from the cliff edge to cross the slopes of Beacon Hill. However, the trail now utilises a section of the England Coast Path, which takes walkers closer to the cliff edge and provides superb views of Staithes, the harbour and Cowbar Nab, with Boulby Cliffs towering behind. The England Coast Path will eventually follow the entire coast of England, and when completed, it will be the world's longest coastal path covering a total distance of around 2795 miles (4498km).

At Port Mulgrave, a forlorn old jetty continues to endure the raging tides in the tiny harbour below. The harbour, which opened in 1857, offered cheaper transportation by sea to take ironstone from the local mines to the blast furnaces at Jarrow on Tyneside, where steel was produced for the shipbuilding industry. Much of the ore came from the Grinkle Park ironstone mine, 3 miles (5km) inland. The ore travelled on a narrow gauge railway which crossed three wooden viaducts and passed through two tunnels to reach Port Mulgrave's harbour. However, during World War I, iron was a vital resource, and once ships left the relative safety of the port, they were in constant danger of attack from German U-boats. Therefore, in 1916, an incline was constructed to connect the Grinkle mine to the Whitby, Redcar and Middlesbrough Union Railway, after that Port Mulgrave became redundant.

The walk continues along the clifftop and follows the headland round to the car park at Runswick Bank Top.

Start/Parking: Runswick Bank Top car park, Bank Top Lane, TS13 5JF.

Location: Runswick Bay is situated off the A174 Thornaby-on-Tees to Whitby road 9 miles (14.5km) north of Whitby.

Grid Ref: NZ 808 161. – **Postcode:** Bank Top Lane, TS13 5JF.

Distance: 7 miles (11.26km) circular. Allow 4 hrs walking time.

Total Ascent: 951 feet (290m). – **Maximum Elevation:** 320 feet (98m).

OS Maps: Explorer OL27 (1:25,000) *North York Moors, Eastern Area* or Landranger 94 (1:50,000) *Whitby and Esk Dale.*

Refreshments: Runswick Bay, Hinderwell, Dalehouse, Staithes and Port Mulgrave.

Public Toilets: Runswick Bay, Hinderwell and Staithes.

Other: Bus service, telephone, Post Office, gift shops, cafes, fish shop, Captain Cook and Staithes Heritage Centre.

(1) 808161 From the car park entrance, opposite the Cliffmount Hotel, turn left and follow the road to the Runswick Bay Hotel. Continue along Hinderwelll Lane and Runswick Lane to the T-junction with the A174 at Hinderwell. **CAUTION: Busy road!**

(2) 794165 Turn right and follow the High Street through the village to the road junction for Port Mulgrave. *(St Hilda's Church and Holy Well are sited on a triangular area of land a short distance from this junction).*

(A) 791169 To visit St Hilda's Church turn right along the side road and follow a path to a gate leading into the churchyard. The Holy Well is sited behind the church. Afterwards return to the main road.

(3) 791169 Cross the High Street and continue down the road opposite *(West End Close).* Turn right into Porret Lane and follow it onto a rougher lane. Turn right and continue to the end of the lane.

(4) 789167 Go over a step stile and continue along a fenced track. Cross another step stile and follow the right fence descending to a step stile at the bottom of the field.

(5) 787166 Cross the step stile, bear right and continue on a narrow fenced path beside the stream. Descend some steps and cross the beck via a wooden footbridge. Ascend the steps opposite and go through a gate, leaving the wood.

(6) 785167 Turn right and continue along the right boundary to cross a step stile leading back into the wood. Bear left and follow a clear track undulating through the wood to a fork.

(7) 784171 Take the left fork and descend to a yellow sign *(Oakridge Nature Reserve - No Hunting),* the path leads down into a clearing with a bench seat. Continue on a stony track to merge with another track descending from the right.

(8) 781175 Continue ahead and descend along a steep track with a steel handrail. At the bottom bear left and cross a wooden bridge *(SP footpath).* Continue ahead on a broad farm lane *(SP Staithes via Dalehouse)* which leads to the main road at Dalehouse. **CAUTION: Busy road!**

(9) 777179 Turn right and follow the road uphill to the A174 main road. **CAUTION: Busy road!** Turn right and continue ascending to the road junction.

(10) 780181 Turn left *(SP Staithes ½)* and follow the road which leads down to Staithes harbour near the Cod and Lobster Inn.

(11) 783188 Turn right into Church Street and follow it uphill onto an enclosed track *(SP Port Mulgrave 1m).* Keep left at a fork and ascend to Fulwood Farm.

(12) 785186 Turn left, go through a gate *(SP Cleveland Way)* and follow a fenced path to the cliff edge. Turn right and continue along the path which leads around the clifftop to a gate.

(13) 792184 Go through the gate, turn left and follow the fence uphill. Pass through another gate *(SP Cleveland Way)* and follow the cliff edge to reach the road near the former coastguard station at Port Mulgrave. Continue along the road.

(14) 796175 Leave the road via a track on the left *(SP Cleveland Way Runswick Bay 2m),* and follow a clear path hugging the clifftop.

(15) 810165 Turn right and follow a clear track to Runswick Bank Top. Turn left *(SP Cleveland Way)* and follow the road to the Cliffmount Hotel and return to the car park.

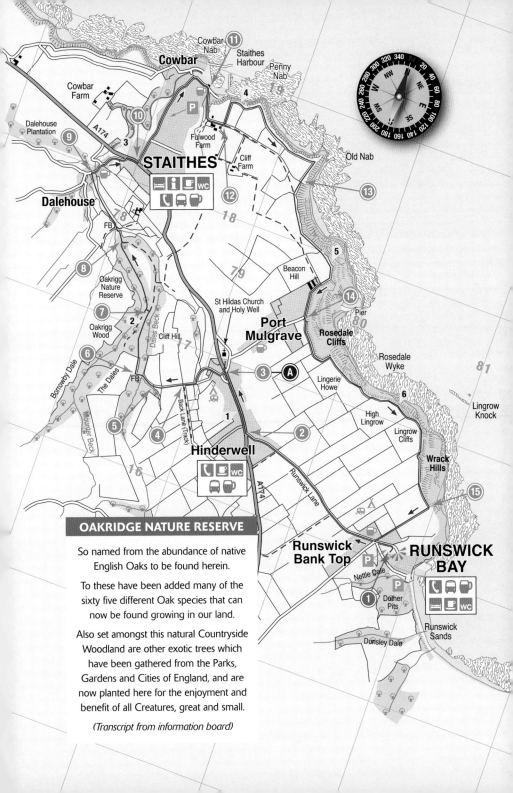

OAKRIDGE NATURE RESERVE

So named from the abundance of native English Oaks to be found herein.

To these have been added many of the sixty five different Oak species that can now be found growing in our land.

Also set amongst this natural Countryside Woodland are other exotic trees which have been gathered from the Parks, Gardens and Cities of England, and are now planted here for the enjoyment and benefit of all Creatures, great and small.

(Transcript from information board)

Kettleness and Goldsborough

FROM RUNSWICK BAY – 7½ MILES (12.07KM)

Runswick Bay Beach and Sailing Club

This walk begins with an enjoyable stroll along golden sands, before ascending to the clifftop to pass around the stunning headland of Kettleness. The route passes the site of a Roman signal station before returning along a disused railway line.

The picturesque village of Runswick Bay nestles at the northern end of a glorious sandy beach, protected by the towering cliff of Lingrow Knowle and some grey stone sea walls. Its narrow pedestrian lanes weave their way between quaint cottages and houses, and on the seafront the former coastguard's cottage is the only remaining thatched house on the Yorkshire coast. In 1682 a landslide swept away the entire village except for one cottage. Nevertheless, there were no casualties because most of the community were attending a funeral wake. One of the mourners realised what was happening and raised the alarm to evacuate the village. Allegedly, the house that survived belonged to the dead man!

Unless the tides are very high, the beach path should be passable. However, beware the caves at Hob Holes, one of which, according to local legend, is the home of the 'Hob of Hob Hole'. In Yorkshire folklore, hobs, goblins, boggles and boggarts are unfriendly sprites with a mischievous nature. But the occupant of the Hob Hole cave had healing powers and could cure whooping cough. Apparently, villagers carried their sick children into the cave and asked for help by the uttering a rhyme – 'Hob Hole Hob, My bairn's gotten t'kink-cough, Tak't off, tak't off.' No one knows what became of the 'Hob of Hob Hole', although some locals still claim that they've seen him lurking around Runswick Bay.

After ascending to High Cliff, we continue along the clifftop, around the dramatic headland of Kettleness. The history of Kettleness provides further evidence of the instability of the coastal cliffs here. On the night of 17 December 1829, torrential rain caused part of the cliff to slide gradually into

28

the sea carrying the entire village with it. Fortunately, the villagers were able to take refuge on an alum ship anchored offshore, and there was no loss of life. The landslide also resulted in the destruction of the alum works located near the shoreline. Although alum production resumed and continued until 1871, the settlement itself never regained its former size.

The path follows a short section of the dismantled Loftus to Whitby Railway line which opened in 1883. The designated course of the line was along the clifftop. Unfortunately, part of the cliff collapsed into the sea during construction and the only alternative was to tunnel through the headlands. The Kettleness tunnel is 308 yards (282m) in length, and after emerging from the cliff, an open section of the track once linked it to the Sandsend tunnel which is 1652 yards (1.51km) long. Please do not consider entering either of these passages, they are unsafe and have not received any maintenance since the line closed in 1958.

A short journey inland leads to the tiny farming community of Goldsborough. Despite its size, the hamlet has an intriguing military history with an RAF radar station and a Roman signal station once sited nearby.

In the early 1950s, RAF Goldsborough was part of the ROTOR air defence radar system, built to provide advanced warning of possible attack by the Soviet Union. The station consisted of a two-storey underground concrete bunker, with a surface guardhouse in the guise of a bungalow, which controlled access to the operations' block. The bungalow, though now derelict and unsafe, is visible from Goldsborough Lane about ¾ mile (1.2km) south-west of the village.

However, the Roman's were here first – in the fourth century AD, they built a signal station on the high ground to the north of the hamlet. Evidently, this station had similar foundations to those at Hunt Cliff (see Walk 1), which suggests that they shared a standard design. The watchtower at Goldsborough would have stood 100 feet (30m) high, with a perimeter wall and a V-shaped ditch providing additional defence. At 425 feet (131m) above sea level, the chosen site provided the sentinels with commanding views along the coastline. The station's principal purpose was to relay messages of impending seaborne attacks to the Roman naval bases in the Humber and Tyne estuaries, and to a cavalry unit at Malton. This well-planned strategy allowed the Romans time to dispatch forces to intercept the invaders.

Leaving the grassy remains behind, we pay a second visit to Kettleness. The building with the distinctive patterned slate roof is the old Kettleness Chapel, founded in 1872 and formerly the mission church of St John the Baptist. Further down the lane is the Kettleness railway station, which closed in 1958 and now operates as an activity centre known as 'Seeonee Lair'; privately owned by the East Cleveland Scouts District.

From Kettleness we follow the route of the dismantled railway, which makes a broad, sweeping curve inland cutting through wooded banks saturated with wildflowers. After passing under four arched bridges, we return to the road near Runswick Bank Top.

The former coastguard's cottage

Start/Parking:	Runswick Bank Top car park, Bank Top Lane, TS13 5JF.
Location:	Runswick Bay is situated off the A174 Thornaby-on-Tees to Whitby road 9 miles (14.5km) north of Whitby.
Grid Ref:	NZ 808 161. – **Postcode:** Bank Top Lane, TS13 5JF.
Distance:	7½ miles (12.07km) circular. Allow 4½ hrs walking time.
Total Ascent:	1187 feet (362m). – **Maximum Elevation:** 482 feet (147m).
OS Maps:	Explorer OL27 (1:25,000) *North York Moors, Eastern Area* or Landranger 94 (1:50,000) *Whitby and Esk Dale.*
Refreshments:	Runswick Bay and Goldsborough.
Public Toilets:	Runswick Bay, none en route.
Other:	Bus service, telephone, cafes.

1 **808161** From the car park entrance, opposite the Cliffmount Hotel, turn right and pass between some concrete posts *(SP Cleveland Way)*. Continue on a steep path which leads down into Runswick Bay. Turn left *(SP Cleveland Way)* and descend along the road to a mini roundabout.

2 **810160** Bear right down the boat slipway leading to the beach and continue along the sands for about ½ mile (800m).

3 **815154** After passing the buildings of the Runswick Bay Sailing Club, turn right and follow Claymoor Beck into a break in the cliffs. Ascend on a stepped path and cross a wooden footbridge. Continue ascending to a welcoming viewpoint seat at High Cliff.

4 **817153** Continue uphill and follow the fence over the summit. Drop down slightly and then ascend to a gate.

5 **823154** Go through the gate and follow the left fence through two more gates. Cross a small dip and ascend some steps. Now continue along the fence to a gate.

6 **829155** Pass through the gate *(SP Cleveland Way)* and follow a farm track to the left. Keep to the left of the farm and head back towards the clifftop. Bear right and follow the fence around the farm emerging onto the minor road.

7 **831156** Turn left and follow the road for about 30 yards (27m). Leave the road via a track on the left *(SP Cleveland Way - Sandsend 3mls)*. Bear right and follow the right fence along the clifftop. Go through a gate and continue along the clifftop to the dismantled railway.

8 **838155** Cross a step stile and climb a few steps. Turn left *(SP Cleveland Way)*, follow the track uphill and go over another step stile. *(The entrance of the Kettleness Tunnel lies just off the track to the right)*. The path now follows the clifftop to Overdale Cliff.

9 **842149** Turn right *(sign Fox and Hounds)* and leave the clifftop. Continue on a broad green track, climbing gradually through three fields to reach the minor road just outside Goldsborough.

10 **840145** Turn right *(sign Fox and Hounds)* and follow the road uphill into Goldsborough, passing the Fox and Hounds. At the road junction, continue ahead and follow the road towards Kettleness *(SP Kettleness)*, for about 100 yards (95m).

11 **835147** Leave the road via a kissing gate on the right *(SP Public Footpath)* and continue along the right boundary, passing around the field corner. Go through another kissing gate and head diagonally left through the field.

12 **834152** Cross a step stile near a derelict barn, bear right and descend through the field to the former mission church of St John the Baptist. Continue over two step stiles and return to the road. Turn right and follow the road into Kettleness.

13 **832155** Leave the road via a gate on the left *(sign Mulgrave Estate)*. This is a permissive path which follows the trackbed of the dismantled railway.

14 **821153** Go through the gate and continue along the permissive path to Ellerby Crossing.

15 **807151** At Ellerby Crossing Cottage continue ahead on a rougher track. Go through a gate, where the track becomes a narrow path which is overgrown in places. Follow the path to the minor road near Runswick Bank Top. **CAUTION: Busy road!**

16 **803156** Turn right and follow the road to the T-junction at Runswick Bank Top. Turn right and continue along the road towards the Cliffmount Hotel, and return to the car park.

Runswick Bank Top

RUNSWICK BAY

Runswick Sands

Low House

Nettle Dale

Dother Pits

Hob Holes

Coverdale Lane

Ellerby Crossing Cottage

Dunsley Dale

Northfields Farm

Barnby Dales

Calais Beck

Claymore Beck

Westfields Farm

Widgey Toft

High Cliff

Claymoor

Barnby Tofts

Brockrigg Farm

Butter Howe

Dismantled Railway

HIGH TIDE

At full tide, the beach between points 2 and 3 is impassable for a few hours. Therefore, check the tide tables and plan your day to allow for this short delay.

Hill Stones

Kettleness Sand

Kettleness Farm

Station

Kettleness

Quarries (disused)

Kettle Ness

Cliff House Farm

Stangoe Carr

Wade's Stone

Whinny Hill

Cow Hill

Goldsborough Lane

Scratch Alley

RAF Goldsborough (site of)

Roman Signal Station (Site of)

Goldsborough

Kettleness Tunnel Entrance (disused)

Scab Nab

Fillet Tail

Holmsgrove Sand

Seaveybog Hill

Overdale Cliff

Line of the Sandend Tunnel

Overdale Farm

Loop Wyke

Telgreen Hill

Lythe

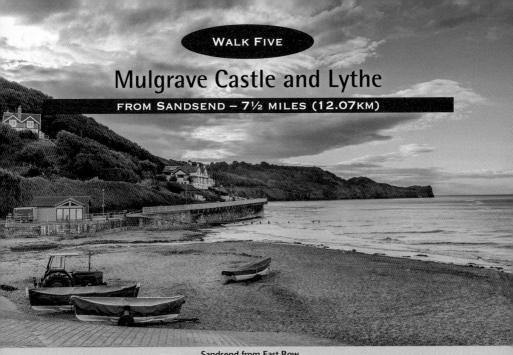

WALK FIVE

Mulgrave Castle and Lythe

FROM SANDSEND – 7½ MILES (12.07KM)

Sandsend from East Row

This exceptionally varied walk ventures into the ancient woods of the Mulgrave Estate. It takes in the ruins of two former castles and then visits the enchanting village of Lythe before returning along the dramatic coastline to Sandsend.

As its name suggests, Sandsend lies at the end of a sandy beach almost 3 miles in length which links the bay with Whitby. Although Sandsend is a picturesque tourist resort nowadays, its origins date back to the seventeenth century, when it had a thriving alum industry which closed in 1871. The village actually consists of two individual hamlets, Sandsend and East Row, connected by a promenade at the foot of Sandsend Rigg. Each settlement lies at the foot of its own beck, which descend through the rich sylvan valleys of the Mulgrave Estate to discharge into the North Sea.

Until the early 1860s, no coast road existed between the village and Whitby. At that time an Indian noble, Duleep Singh, the last Maharajah of the Sikh Empire, was the tenant of Mulgrave Castle. The Maharajah

constructed the first road from Sandsend to Whitby. According to tradition, he had the road built because his elephants didn't enjoy walking on the beach. However, there is no evidence of elephants being kept at the castle.

From the car park, we follow the road along the seafront to East Row, The route then continues into the Mulgrave Estate, passing the remains of a Roman cement works. The cement produced here was nothing like any substance used by the Romans. The mill opened in 1811 and processed large calcareous nodules found in the upper levels of the alum shale on Sandsend Ness. After roasting the nodules in a kiln, they were ground to a fine powder – Roman cement. When made into a mortar with sand, the product set in five-to-fifteen minutes. In the nineteenth century, Roman cement was invaluable for its ability to set rapidly even underwater; hence it was indispensable in the construction of piers, docks and marine defences. The cement works carried on production until 1933, with tunnels gouged into the cliffs to extract the calcareous nodules. The mill is now a private dwelling, and although the wheel pit survives, the wheel itself has gone. The calcining kiln sited to the rear of the mill building remains virtually intact.

The track winds its way through Mulgrave Woods, ascending along the sylvan valley of East Row Beck, which flourishes with an abundance of native flora and fauna. In spring woodland flowers, such as bluebell, primrose, violet, wild garlic and wood anenome are prolific, hastening to blossom before the canopy closes over and blocks out the sun. The woods also provide refuge to many wild creatures, with mammals such as badger, roe deer, squirrel, stoat and weasel as well as numerous species of birds breeding here.

At the head of the valley, we reach the extensive ruins of the old Mulgrave Castle, which dates from the early twelfth century. The castle's elevated position on a narrow ridge, between two deep valleys with swift flowing streams, made it very difficult to attack; therefore it was strategically important. At the outbreak of the English Civil War in 1642, the Royalist forces seized the castle and strengthened its fortifications. Consequently, in 1647 Parliament issued orders to render the castle untenable; thus crumbling towers and broken walls are all that remain of this once magnificent fortress.

On the perimeter of the wood, 850 yards (770m) west of the old castle, is the site of Foss Castle – Mulgrave's precursor. This was a motte-and-bailey fortification, founded c. 1072 to assert Norman rule following the aftermath of the 'Harrying of the North' by William the Conqueror. The motte is visible to the right of the track.

After leaving Mulgrave Woods, we ascend through beautiful countryside to the peaceful hamlet of East Barnby. The route continues onto a wooded ridge which provides open views towards Whitby Abbey.

Carrying on through the fields we arrive at Lythe, which maintains the ancient custom of 'Firing the Stiddy' to signal notable events such as the Queen's Jubilee. The Stiddy is an upturned anvil originally sited outside the blacksmith's shop. After packing the base with gunpowder, the charge is set-off by the heated tip of a long iron bar, and a loud explosion follows. One of the most recent firing's took place on 22 May 2018, to commemorate the royal wedding of Prince Harry and Meghan Markle.

Just outside the village, stands St Oswald's Church, which houses an informative display of Anglo-Scandinavian carved stones – relics of a tenth-century cemetery. These artefacts, recovered from the walls and buttresses during the 1910 restoration confirm that a Christian church has stood here since at least AD 950. One of Lythe's former vicars was John Fisher, who later became a cardinal. However, during the Reformation, Fisher refused to accept King Henry VIII as the Supreme Head of the Church of England, which led to his execution for treason in 1535. This brutal act validated Fisher's beatification as a martyr in 1886, and his canonisation in 1935 – four hundred years after his death.

Spiritually refreshed, we press on towards the coastal cliffs, where we merge with the Cleveland Way. From here the route follows the headland round, before dropping down into Overdale Wood. After a steep descent, we join the trackbed of the dismantled Loftus to Whitby Railway line near the Sandsend tunnel entrance.

The trackbed winds its way between the old Deepgrove and Sandsend alum quarries which were in use from 1605 to 1867. Although the scars left by this former industry still resemble a lunar landscape, they are slowly healing, and the quarry workings and spoil heaps now provide a variety of habitats for wildlife. Moreover, this bleak wasteland, after being appropriately whitened by computer graphics, appeared as part of the Antarctic landscape in the 2012 film *Shackleton* which starred Sir Kenneth Branagh.

During the return to Sandsend, we take advantage of the level surface underfoot, which allows us to appreciate the inspiring coastal scenery.

Start/Parking: Sandsend car park, at the foot of Lythe Bank, YO21 3TD.

Location: Sandsend is situated on the A174 Thornaby-on-Tees to Whitby road 3 miles (4.8km) north of Whitby.

Grid Ref: NZ 860129. – **Postcode:** YO21 3TD.

Distance: 7½ miles (12.07km) circular. Allow 4½ hrs walking time.

Total Ascent: 1041 feet (317m). – **Maximum Elevation:** 618 feet (188m).

OS Maps: Explorer OL27 (1:25,000) *North York Moors, Eastern Area* or Landranger 94 (1:50,000) *Whitby and Esk Dale.*

Refreshments: Sandsend and Lythe.

Public Toilets: Sandsend.

Other: Bus service, telephone, Post Office, gift shops, cafes, fish shop.

ACCESS TO MULGRAVE WOODS

NB: The woods are only open to the public on Wednesdays, Saturdays, Sundays and Bank Holidays throughout the year except for the month of May when they are closed for the entire month.

(1) 860129 Turn left onto the A174 main road and follow it along the promenade to the bridge at East Row. **CAUTION: busy road!**

(2) 862125 Do not cross the bridge, leave the road and enter the Mulgrave Estate. Head towards the rear of the car park and follow the estate lane to some wooden buildings.

(3) 858122 Pass between the buildings and follow the stony track to a small wooden hut.

(4) 849119 Take the left fork and continue to another junction of tracks.

(5) 846118 Bear left and remain above the beck to a junction with a green metal bench.

(6) 841117 Continue along the left fork. Leave the track via some steps on the right, which lead up to the castle entrance. **CAUTION: DO NOT climb on the walls.** *(This also applies to any children with you!)*

(7) 839117 After viewing the castle remains return to the entrance, turn right and follow the track to a junction. Continue directly ahead on a narrower path, ascending to a gate at the woodland edge.

(8) 832116 Go through the smaller gate on the right *(SP Footpath),* turn right and descend to a gate. Pass through the gate and cross the ford. **CAUTION: if the beck is in spate, please retrace your steps to** point 8 **and use option A.**

(9) 830117 Bear right and ascend to some derelict stone buildings. Continue along a broad track, *(passing Mulgrave's motte and bailey castle)* and join an enclosed farm lane leading to the road near High Leas. Turn right and continue towards the farmhouse.

(10) 829121 Go through a gateway on the left, opposite the farmhouse *(SP Public Footpath).* Follow the right boundary and pass through a small wood. Cross a step stile and continue along the right boundary to the road at East Barnby. Turn right and follow the road uphill into the village.

(11) 827126 Leave the road via a green track on the right *(SP Public Footpath),* pass between the cottages and go through a gate. Continue over two stiles and pass through a small wood.

(12) 829126 Turn left and follow a fenced track along the edge of the woodland.

(13) 842129 At the woodland edge go through two gates, turn left and follow the boundary around the sportsground. Go through a gate and turn right onto the A174 main road. **CAUTION: busy road!** Follow the road through Lythe to St. Oswald's Church.

NB: To visit the church, continue along the roadside path to a gate leading into the churchyard.

(14) 849131 Turn left, follow the lane to the bend and go through a waymarked gate. Continue along the right hedge, pass through a gate and follow an enclosed green lane leading into Overdale Wood.

(15) 846139 Follow a clear track through the wood, go through a gate, bear left and climb uphill to Overdale Farm. Pass between the farm buildings and head to the corner of the field.

(16) 847143 Turn right and follow the left boundary through the field. Turn left *(SP Public Footpath)* and continue to Telgreen Hill. Turn right *(SP Cleveland Way - Sandsend)* and follow the clifftop path.

(17) 851146 Leave the clifftop and follow the right boundary downhill to the entrance of a wood.

(18) 854142 Enter the wood via a gate and descend some steep wooden and stone steps. **CAUTION: the steps are very steep and often slippery!** Turn left and join the dismantled railway line near the Sandsend Tunnel entrance. Follow the trackbed for about 1 mile (1.6km). *(Leaving the National Park).*

(19) 859130 Leave the trackbed via a narrow path on the left, descend some steps and return to the car park at Sandsend.

15

Overdale Wyke

Keldhowe Steel

Deepgrove Wyke

Sandsend Ness

Sandsend

87

⑰

⑱

⑲

Loop Wyke

Telgreen Hill

6

Sandsend Tunnel Entrance (disused)

7

①

②

East Row

Overdale Cliff

Sandsend Beach

Line of the Sandend Tunnel

Overdale Farm

Deepgrove Farm

A174

86

National Park Boundary

⑯

⑮

St Oswald's Church

SANDSEND

Saw Mill

Ford

③

5

⑭

Tigh na Bruaich

Weir

LYTHE

13

Sandsend Beck

Weir

FB

85

1

Brake End Plantation

Upton Hall Farm

Mulgrave Castle

Hell Scar

④

⑬

The Park

Weir

4

Cow Pasture Plantation

84

Ford

Weir

FB

⑤

A174

Wade's Stone

Ash Holm

FB

Weir

⑫

FB

PB Ford

⑥

East Row Beck

Nineteen Lands

FB

Mulgrave Castle

Steps

FB

2

⑦

83

FB

East Barnby

3

High Leas

FB

Ford

⑪

Motte

⑩

Ford

82

⑨

Weir

West Barnby

Barnby Sleights

Ⓐ ⑧

Ⓑ

1-1

ALTERNATIVE ROUTE

NB: Please use this route if the beck at **point 9** is in spate.

Ⓐ **832116** Cross the stile, turn right and follow an enclosed track. Go through a gate and follow the left boundary to Barnby Sleights Farm. Enter the farmyard, turn right and follow the farm lane to the minor road.

Ⓑ **823116** Turn right and follow the road downhill to a crossroads. At the junction, continue directly across and follow the road uphill to East Barnby.

Whitby and East Row

FROM WHITBY – 7½ MILES (12.07KM)

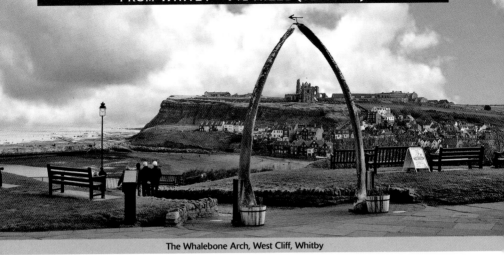

The Whalebone Arch, West Cliff, Whitby

This scenic ramble incorporates a variety of visually appealing features. Providing the tide is receding, the walk concludes with a relaxing stroll along the sandy beach – followed by a trip into the Khyber Pass!

The Anglo-Saxon name for Whitby was Streonshalh, which the Venerable Bede interpreted as 'Sinus Fari' meaning 'the bay of the light'. In AD 655 Oswy, the Christian king of Northumbria, defeated Penda, the pagan king of Mercia, at the Battle of Winwaid. To commemorate his victory, he endowed the first monastery here, founded in AD 657 by the Abbess Hilda (see Walk 7). At the time of the Norman Conquest in 1066, the abbey was in ruins, although there was a sizeable village known as Whitby in the harbour below. The town's name derives from old Norse and translates as 'white settlement', possibly referring to the brightness of the newly built dwellings at that time.

The early part of the walk passes through Whitby's sprawling suburbs, embracing the beautiful gardens of Pannett Park. In addition

to being a haven of peace and tranquillity, the park is home to the Pannett Art Gallery and Whitby Museum. The museum contains many impressive collections and artefacts of local and national interest. It also houses the only known 'Hand of Glory' still in existence – the severed hand of a hanged man, (see *Miscellanea* page 56). The hand supposedly possesses special magical properties!

Standing on the outskirts of the town is the nineteenth-century Sneaton Castle, built for James Wilson, who had accumulated considerable wealth from his sugar plantations in the West Indies – where he used slave labour. The slave registers for 1817 show that Wilson had 340 slaves working on his estates. However, with the abolition of slavery looming, Wilson moved to Whitby and set about becoming a pillar of respectable society. In 1826 he became the MP for York. His first Parliamentary speech opposed the immediate emancipation of slaves.

In 1915 Sneaton Castle became the home of the Anglican Order of the Holy Paraclete, who founded the adjacent St Hilda's Priory;

the term Paraclete refers to the Holy Spirit. The order used the castle as a girls' boarding school until 1997, when it re-opened as a conference and study centre. At present, a new priory is being built in the castle grounds to relocate the order.

Leaving suburbia behind, we now enjoy more peaceful rural settings, passing through the hamlets of Newholm and Dunsley to reach the golden beach at Sandsend.

Ye Olde Beehive Inne at Newholm is a former drovers' inn, one of the many regular stopping places along drove roads, known as stances. These usually had an inn with an overnight pound and essential grazing for herds of cattle en route to the market towns of Malton and York.

Neighbouring Dunsley's main attraction is the Dunsley Hall Country House Hotel, built in 1900 as a holiday home for a Victorian shipping magnate. Early records for this tiny hamlet suggest that the Romans landed in Dunsley Bay – the 'Dunum Sinus' of Ptolemy, now called Sandsend Bay. The Danes reputedly landed at Dunsley Bay in AD 867 with a sizeable army and placed their banner depicting a raven upon the hill, known since that time as 'Raven Hill'.

After descending through an enchanting wooded ravine, we arrive at East Row and the enticing Sandsend Beach. Providing the tide is out, we can continue along the sands; otherwise, it's safer to follow the road – both options lead to Whitby's West Cliff.

The whalebone arch on the West Cliff is a memorial to the whaling industry. The 15-foot jaw bones came from a bowhead whale, legally killed by Alaskan Inuits in 1996, and unveiled by Miss Alaska in 2003. Two other arches have stood on the same spot; in 1963 Norway presented Whitby with some 20-foot jawbones from a fin whale to replace the original arch, erected c.1853, which was in terrible condition.

Whaling played a significant role in the town's growth and prosperity. In 1753 the first two ships of the newly formed Whitby Whaling Company set sail for Greenland.

By 1795 Whitby had become a significant whaling port, with fifty-five vessels operating from the harbour. Large boiler houses sited along the quayside rendered the whale blubber into oil used for street lighting; or utilised in the production of candles, soap, margarine and paint. However, the introduction of gas lighting reduced the demand for whale oil products, and by 1831 just one whaling ship remained. The end of Whitby's whaling industry came in 1837, and the last whaling ship that returned to the harbour was empty.

One of the most successful captains was William Scoresby Senior (1760-1829). During his career, he made thirty voyages and caught a total of 533 whales – the highest number anywhere in Europe. In 1807, he invented the 'crow's nest', which provided shelter for lookouts at the top of the masthead. According to tradition, the three-tier pulpit in St. Mary's Church inspired its design.

Besides its maritime history, Whitby is also well-known for its high-quality jet; a hard, black variety of lignite, derived from fossilised wood, which has endured tremendous pressure over millions of years. Although the history of jet dates back to at least the Bronze Age, it was during the Victorian period that Whitby Jet achieved popularity. Following the death of her consort, Prince Albert, in 1861, Queen Victoria began an extended period of mourning. Thus, the Queen decreed that only jewellery fashioned from jet was acceptable to wear at Court, thus confirming jet's status as the material of choice for jewellery during times of mourning.

From the memorial, we descend onto the 'Khyber Pass', which leads down to the harbour and piers. This road takes its name from the mountain pass on the border of Pakistan and Afghanistan. Fortunately, the conclusion of our journey is much closer! Nevertheless, before returning to the car park, you may wish to explore the waterfront or visit some of the artists' studios and jet jewellery shops; or perhaps a portion of tasty fish and chips is more tempting!

Start/Parking:	Whitby from the Endeavour Wharf car park, YO21 1YW.
Location:	Whitby is situated off the A171 Middlesbrough to Scarborough road 19 miles (30.5km) north of Scarborough.
Grid Ref:	NZ 899107. – **Postcode:** YO213TD.
Distance:	7½ miles (12.07km) circular. Allow 4½ hrs walking time.
Total Ascent:	900 feet (274m). – **Maximum Elevation:** 370 feet (113m).
OS Maps:	Explorer OL27 (1:25,000) *North York Moors, Eastern Area* or Landranger 94 (1:50,000) *Whitby and Esk Dale.*
Refreshments:	Whitby, Newholm, East Row and Sandsend.
Public Toilets:	Whitby and Sandsend.
Other:	Bus service, telephone, Post Office, gift shops, cafes, fish shops, museums.

1 899107 Leave the car park and turn left at the roundabout. Pass the railway and bus stations, continue across Victoria Square onto Bagdale, ascend along the road to Pannett Park.

2 895108 Leave the road and climb some steps leading into the park, follow the left fork and pass to the left of the museum. Exit the park via a gate beside the playground.

NB: Dogs are not permitted in the park, so dog owners should continue along the road to the roundabout, turn right and follow Chubb Hill Road to point 3.

3 894110 Drop down slightly to the left and cross the road, ascend back towards the roundabout and turn left onto Spring Vale. Follow the road uphill onto Stakesby Road and at a left bend join Castle Road.

4 884107 Turn right and follow the road uphill passing Sneaton Castle and St Hilda's Priory.

5 877105 Leave the road *(SP Footpath)*, follow the right boundary and cross a step stile. Now follow the left boundary through three fields.

6 869105 Cross the road and the stile opposite *(SP Footpath)*, follow the right boundary and cross a step stile. Head directly across the field towards a static caravan. Cross another step stile and pass between the cottages to reach the road. Turn right and follow the road to Ye Olde Beehive Inne.

7 867106 After passing the inn, leave the road via a lane on the left. Bear right along Howlgate Lane and follow it to a cottage – The Green.

8 865107 Leave the lane via a gate opposite the cottage *(SP Footpath)*, follow the left boundary, descending to cross a step stile *(Waymark)*. At a fork bear left and continue descending to a footbridge.

9 864109 Cross the footbridge and ascend the steps opposite. Follow the right boundary over the crest to an old stone gate post. Turn left and follow the raised track through the field.

10 861109 Turn right and head directly across the field. Enter the wood and follow a faint path leading down to a footbridge. Cross the footbridge, ascend some steps and cross a stile. Continue ahead climbing steeply towards the top right field corner.

11 858109 Go through a gate onto the road, turn right and follow the road over the crest passing the Dunsley Hall Hotel. Descend to a T-junction, turn right *(SP Sandsend 1½m)* and follow the road downhill for about 550 yards (500m). **CAUTION: busy road!**

12 861115 Leave the road via some steps on the left banking *(SP Footpath)* and go through a kissing gate. Bear half left, continue across two fields and go through a kissing gate. Bear left, descending towards the right boundary and a step stile.

13 861119 Cross the stile and follow the left hedge, near the bottom of the field bear right and go through a wooden gate. Follow the left boundary, cross a step stile and descend through the wood. Exit the wood via two more step stiles. Turn right onto a rough lane leading to the bridge at East Row.

14 862125 Turn right and follow the A174 main road for about 1¼ miles (2km). **CAUTION: busy road!**

An alternative beach route between points 14 and 18 is shown in the blue panel opposite.

15 879116 After passing the Whitby Golf Club leave the main road via a narrow lane on the left *(SP Cleveland Way)*.

16 881119 Bear right and ascend a narrower path leading to the clifftop. Continue on a good path along the clifftop and return to the road near West Cliff.

17 891115 Follow the road to the Captain Cook statue overlooking the harbour.

18 897114 Pass through the Whalebone Arch and descend the path into the Khyber Pass. Turn left, follow the road downhill around a double bend and continue onto Pier Road.

19 898114 Follow the road beside the pier to the swing bridge at Bridge Street. Continue across the road to the roundabout, turn left and return into the Endeavour Wharf car park.

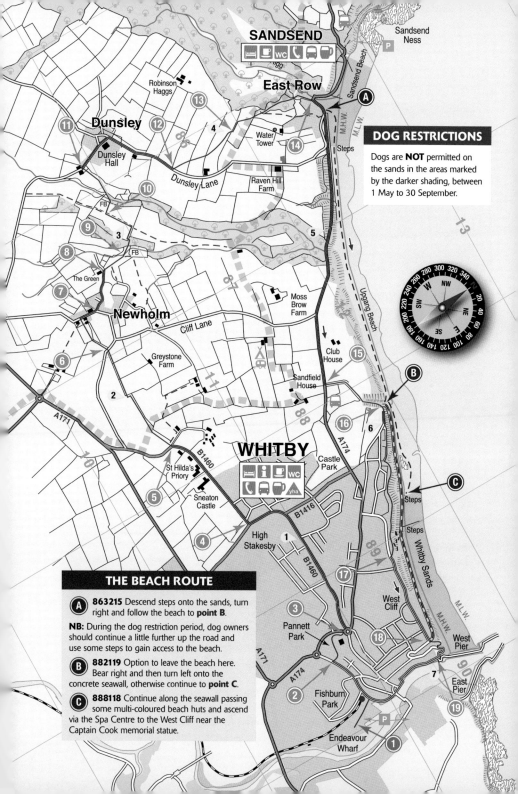

DOG RESTRICTIONS

Dogs are **NOT** permitted on the sands in the areas marked by the darker shading, between 1 May to 30 September.

THE BEACH ROUTE

Ⓐ **863215** Descend steps onto the sands, turn right and follow the beach to **point B**.

NB: During the dog restriction period, dog owners should continue a little further up the road and use some steps to gain access to the beach.

Ⓑ **882119** Option to leave the beach here. Bear right and then turn left onto the concrete seawall, otherwise continue to **point C**.

Ⓒ **888118** Continue along the seawall passing some multi-coloured beach huts and ascend via the Spa Centre to the West Cliff near the Captain Cook memorial statue.

The Larpool Viaduct and Whitby Abbey

FROM LOW HAWSKER – 8 MILES (12.9KM)

Steam train passing under the Larpool Viaduct

Whether your interests lie in history and culture, vampires and Goths, or just fish and chips – this walk ticks all those boxes. First, a gentle stroll leads to the Larpool Viaduct where we cross the river Esk. Then after enjoying some of Whitby's many attractions, a bracing clifftop walk leads back to Hawsker.

Leaving Hawsker, we follow a section of the Scarborough and Whitby railway path, also known as the 'Cinder Track', because it used cinders as ballast, rather than crushed stone. The track leads to the Larpool Viaduct, an imposing and picturesque structure, which stands to the west of Whitby's town centre. The viaduct is 915 feet (279m) in length with thirteen arches supported by twelve pillars, and the longest span is 64 feet (19.5m), crossing the middle of the river at the height of 120 feet (36.5m). Moreover, it

reputedly comprises five million red bricks. The construction took two years, finishing on 24 October 1884. The line opened in July 1885. It followed a challenging but scenic route along the North Yorkshire coast from Scarborough to Whitby and survived until March 1965, a victim of the Beeching Axe.

From the viaduct, we descend to cross the Esk Valley Railway line, which shares the track with steam trains from the North Yorkshire Moors Railway. The line was another victim of the Beeching cuts. However, the North York Moors Historical Railway Trust reopened the track in 1973, and now it is a very popular 18 mile (29km) heritage railway.

Although Whitby is probably most famous for its fishing and whaling fleets, its economy now relies more on tourism than industry. However, during the latter part of the eighteenth century, Whitby was England's

40

third largest shipbuilding centre after London and Newcastle, with eleven shipyards along the river Esk. Whitby's shipbuilding industry is especially famous for its collier-barks, known as Whitby Cats; three-masted sailing ships designed for carrying coal. These sturdy boats had flat-bottomed keels, enabling them to land on beaches to load and unload their cargoes, and also made repairs and maintenance simple. These features made them popular with the explorers of the day, including the celebrated Captain James Cook; all four of his vessels were Whitby built collier ships. A full-scale replica of HM *Bark Endeavour*, the vessel which Cook used during his first voyage of discovery in 1768, now forms part of a tourist attraction in Endeavour Wharf. (For more information on Captain Cook and his voyages see *Miscellanea* page 60).

The Irish author, Bram Stoker, conceived the idea for his classic novel *Dracula* in Whitby. In 1890 while staying at a guest house here, he read about the shipwreck of a Russian vessel named the *Dmitry*, from Narva. The ship ran aground in 1885 on Tate Hill Sands carrying a cargo of silvery sand. After a slight modification of the name, this became the *Demeter* from Varna. It brings Dracula to Whitby with a shipment of silver sand and boxes of earth from Transylvania. Immediately after the *Demeter* ran aground, an enormous black dog leapt ashore and bounded up the steps towards Whitby Abbey – Dracula had arrived! However, Stoker spent six more years researching the scenery and traditions of Transylvania, and the name of his villain, before publishing his novel. Nevertheless, his holiday in Whitby inspired some of the novel's most dramatic scenes.

Leaving Whitby, the route ascends the 199 steps, known locally as the Church Stairs. Every tenth step and the last one has a small brass plate denoting the step number - so at least you don't have to count them!

In the graveyard of St Mary's Church, the Cædmon Cross pays tribute to the talented seventh-century poet. According to the Venerable Bede, Cædmon was a lay brother at Whitby Abbey, where he cared for the animals. One evening while he was sleeping, Cædmon had a vision, inspiring him to compose a short poem praising God and the creation, which he sang to the Abbess Hilda. Subsequently, Cædmon joined the monastic community where he became an enthusiastic monk and an inspirational Christian poet.

The Abbess Hilda, also known as Hild and later St Hilda, was a Northumbrian princess; she founded the first monastery here in AD 657. The abbey soon became one of the most revered religious centres in the Anglo-Saxon world. In AD 664 it was the setting for the Synod of Whitby, to decide whether the Church should adopt the Celtic or Roman method for calculating the date of the movable Easter feast. The Synod voted in favour of the Roman system – a landmark in the history of the Church in England and this contributed to a decline in Celtic Christianity.

Towards the end of the ninth century Danish invaders laid waste to the area and the abbey fell into disuse. However, c.1078 after a lapse of two centuries, Reinfrid, a Benedictine monk who had been a fearless soldier in the army of William the Conqueror, founded a new monastic community on the same site. The crown confiscated Whitby Abbey and all its possessions in 1539 during Henry VIII's Dissolution of the Monasteries. In December 1914, German battleships shelled Whitby and the west front of the abbey sustained considerable damage.

From the abbey, the path follows the clifftop to Saltwick Bay. In October 1914, the hospital ship SS *Rohilla* sank in the bay near Saltwick Nab. Although weather conditions made the rescue extremely difficult, 146 of the 229 on board survived, including the captain and all the nurses. One of the survivors was Mary Kezia Roberts who had survived the sinking of the RMS *Titanic* in 1912.

The path continues along the clifftop, passing around the former fog signal station and lighthouse at Ling Hill. After leaving the coastline, we head inland to rejoin the Cinder Track and return to Hawsker.

Start/Parking: Low Hawsker Village Hall car park or the adjacent lay-by.

Location: Low Hawsker is situated on the A171 Whitby to Scarborough road 3 miles (4.8km) south of Whitby.

Grid Ref: NZ 925 077. – **Postcode:** Mill Lane, Low Hawsker – YO22 4LT.

Distance: 8 miles (12.9km) circular. Allow 4½ hrs walking time.

Total Ascent: 1178 feet (359m). – **Maximum Elevation:** 372 feet (113m).

OS Maps: Explorer OL27 (1:25,000) *North York Moors, Eastern Area* or Landranger 94 (1:50,000) *Whitby and Esk Dale.*

Refreshments: Stainsacre, Hawsker and Whitby.

Public Toilets: Whitby: Car parks at Endeavour Wharf and Church Street.

Other: Bus service, Trailways Cycle Hire, telephone, Youth Hostel.

Alternative Start: Whitby from the Endeavour Wharf car park, YO21 1YW – see blue panel.

1 925077 Follow the road towards Whitby. Just after passing the pedestrian crossing leave the road via a gate on the left and follow the dismantled railway line to the bridge at Stainsacre.

2 913085 Continue across the bridge and follow the trackway to the Larpool Viaduct.

3 896095 Cross the viaduct and follow the track around the bend to a junction of paths near a signpost.

4 895099 Turn right *(SP Whitby)* and follow a fenced footpath *(SP Esk Valley Walk).* Pass to the left of the Airy Hill Holiday Park *(Waymark)* and continue towards the main road.

5 897102 Before reaching the main road take a footpath on the right which passes around the playing field. When the path forks, follow the right path, descend some steps and pass underneath the main road. Climb back up, turn right and descend along a tarmac path.

6 898103 Turn right and follow the road for about 30 yards (27m). Take a rough track on the right *(Waymark Esk Valley Walk).* Continue to cross the railway via the crossing. **DANGER: STOP, LOOK, LISTEN before crossing the railway line!** Bear left and follow the footpath along the quayside through the car park.

7 899109 Leave the car park, turn right and follow the road to the swing bridge, *(passing the replica of HM Bark Endeavour).* Cross the bridge and continue along Bridge Street into the old town.

8 900111 Turn left into Church Street and follow the cobbled street. Turn right and ascend the 199 steps to St Mary's Church. Continue along the road passing the entrance to Whitby Abbey.

9 903113 Turn left *(SP Cleveland Way - Robin Hood's Bay 6½m)* and head to the cliff edge. Turn right and follow a fenced path along the clifftop.

10 912111 Descend some steps, bear right and follow a rough track into the static caravan park. Turn left and follow the road through the site.

11 915107 When the road leaves the caravan park bear left and go through a gate *(SP Cleveland Way - Robin Hood's Bay 5m).* Follow a good path along the clifftop to Whitestone Point.

12 926103 Continue along the clifftop passing the Whitby fog signal station.

13 928102 Turn right, climb uphill and go through a gate *(SP Cleveland Way).* Cross the service road and ascend some steps. Go through a gate *(SP Cleveland Way)* and pass above the lighthouse. Continue along the clifftop, passing High Whitby and Widdy Head to reach a memorial seat.

14 934091 Descend some steps and cross a stream. Ascend some more steps, returning to the clifftop and continue to a signpost.

15 937086 Leave the clifftop via a step stile on the right *(SP Hawsker 1m)* and ascend steeply beside the wall. At the corner of the wall near the summit, bear right *(SP Hawsker)* and go through a gate *(Waymark).* Turn left, pass through a gate and follow the farm lane to a bridge leading over the dismantled railway. **DON'T cross the bridge.**

16 927078 Just before the bridge go through a metal gate on the left, descend some steps and turn right rejoining the Cinder Track. Pass under the bridge and follow the trackway to the main road. **CAUTION: Busy road!** Cross the road via the pedestrian crossing, turn left and return to the car park.

DIRECTIONS FOR WHITBY START

A 899109 Park in the Endeavour Wharf car park. Return to the car park entrance and follow the sequential directions given from **point 7** to **16**.

B 925078 Cross the main road via the pedestrian crossing, turn right, after a few yards turn left and go through a gate. Continue along the Cinder Track to **point 2** and then use the sequential directions given to **point 7**.

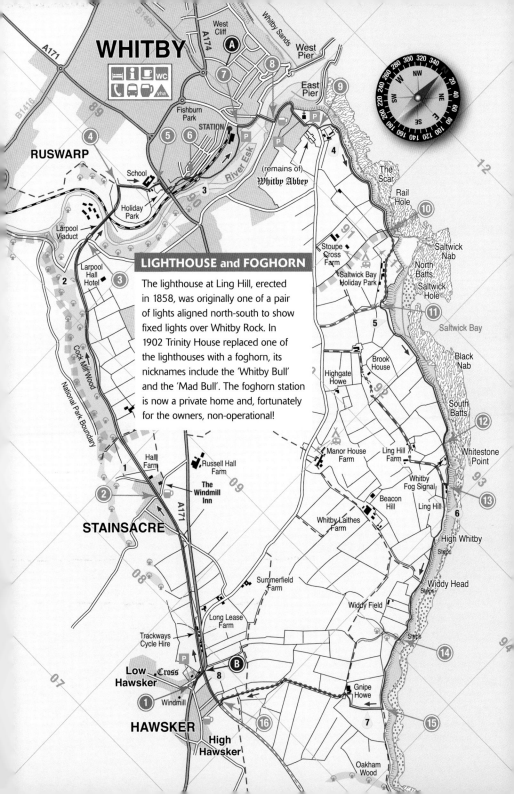

WHITBY

RUSWARP

West Cliff

West Pier

East Pier

Whitby Sands

Fishburn Park

STATION

School

Holiday Park

Larpool Viaduct

Larpool Hall Hotel

River Esk

(remains of)
Whitby Abbey

The Scar

Rail Hole

Saltwick Nab

North Batts

Saltwick Hole

Stoupe Cross Farm

Saltwick Bay Holiday Park

Saltwick Bay

Black Nab

South Batts

Brook House

Highgate Howe

Whitestone Point

Ling Hill Farm

Manor House Farm

Whitby Fog Signal

Beacon Hill

Ling Hill

High Whitby

Widdy Head

Widdy Field

Whitby Laithes Farm

National Park Boundary

Cock Mill Wood

Hall Farm

Russell Hall Farm

The Windmill Inn

STAINSACRE

Summerfield Farm

Long Lease Farm

Trackways Cycle Hire

Low Hawsker

Cross

Windmill

HAWSKER

High Hawsker

Gnipe Howe

Oakham Wood

LIGHTHOUSE and FOGHORN

The lighthouse at Ling Hill, erected in 1858, was originally one of a pair of lights aligned north-south to show fixed lights over Whitby Rock. In 1902 Trinity House replaced one of the lighthouses with a foghorn, its nicknames include the 'Whitby Bull' and the 'Mad Bull'. The foghorn station is now a private home and, fortunately for the owners, non-operational!

Maw Wyke Hole and Robin Hood's Bay

FROM LOW HAWSKER – 7¾ MILES (12.47KM)

Millennium Statue, Robin Hood's Bay

This scenic walk visits the enchanting Robin Hood's Bay, a former smugglers' haunt and home to a wealth of historical and cultural interest. After exploring the town, an inland route leads us back through the fields to Hawsker.

The village of Hawsker consists of two parts, known as High and Low, and it formerly had a cobbler, tailor, blacksmith and a windmill. Of these only the mill at Low Hawsker remains. The mill, built c.1861, stood 64 feet (19.5m) in height with three storeys and four sails, it remained in use until around 1915, and the removal of the upper levels took place in 1960.

Standing in an enclosure further along the road is the shaft of Hawsker Cross, which is an excellent example of a tenth-century Anglo-Saxon wayside cross. The cross is visible from the lane and comprises a stone base, split into two halves near the socket hole, and a shaft broken off just below the head. Apart from strengthening the faith of passing Christians, wayside crosses also served as waymarkers to reassure travellers. These often marked long-distance routes, especially those used for pilgrimages or serving a particular religious purpose, such as access to church services or funeral processions.

From Hawsker, we follow a short section of the Cinder Track to join the Coast to Coast Walk, which descends to the clifftop and merges with the Cleveland Way. The nearby inlet of Maw Wyke Hole is nationally significant for its rich assemblage of fern fossils – possible remnants of thick marshy vegetation. It also provides valuable nesting sites for a variety of seabirds, including cormorants, fulmars, kittiwakes and herring gulls. Anticipate a raucous welcome!

The path from Maw Wyke Hole clings to the clifftop, undulating along the spectacular coastline with its dramatic cliffs and rocks.

After passing around the headland of Ness Point, the broad sweep of Robin Hood's Bay suddenly comes into view, curving gracefully towards the rugged peninsular at Ravenscar some three miles away.

Just beyond the viewpoint, we pass into the aptly named Rocket Post Field. The post standing in this field, which simulated a ship's mast and crow's nest, is a replica of the one formerly used by coastguard rescue teams to practice ship to shore rescues. When a vessel became stranded, the rescuers fired a rocket, with a rope attached to it, over the stricken vessel. The crew then secured the line to a substantial part of their ship, usually the main mast, and a 'breeches buoy' carried the crew ashore one at a time. A breeches buoy is merely a pair of canvas shorts attached to a circular cork lifebuoy, hanging from a rope.

On 25 January 1936, SS *Heatherfield* ran aground at Ness Point in a foggy haze and at low tide. By the time the rocket reached the ship, several people had already swum ashore, but the majority used the breeches buoy. The captain observed tradition and was the last person to leave the ship, giving a resounding cheer as he reached the safety of the clifftop. He was carrying his pet canary in a cage!

Leaving the rocket post behind, we press on to Robin Hood's Bay. The narrow cobbled main street descends steeply to Bay Town, which is the local name for the lower and most picturesque part of the village. A massive concrete seawall, constructed in 1975, protects the town from the wrath of the North Sea and has helped to slow down coastal erosion. Nonetheless, at high tide when the waves pound against the seawalls and surge over the slipway, the surf often encroaches into the bottom of the main street. The seawall also serves as a promenade and features a mosaic 165 foot (50m) in length celebrating events relevant to 'The Bay'.

The first written record for Robin Hood's Bay was in 1536 when King Henry VIII's topographer, John Leland, described it as 'a fisher townlet of twenty boats'. However, the origin of its name is unknown, and there is no evidence that the legendary Robin Hood of Sherwood Forest ever visited the bay. The name probably arose from a variety of legends and may refer to Robin (in the) Hood, an ancient forest sprite similar to Robin Goodfellow, a more familiar name used for comparable elves and fairies across the country. Apparently, he haunted the barrows on the moor above. Moreover, Robin Goodfellow was the alter-ego of Puck, that mischievous imp of English folklore, immortalised in William Shakespeare's play – *A Midsummer Night's Dream.*

A plaque in the village acknowledges a spectacular rescue and records:

On the 18th January 1881, the Brig 'Visitor' ran ashore at Robin Hood's Bay. No local boat could be launched on account of the violence of the storm, so the Whitby lifeboat was brought overland past this point – a distance of 6 miles – through snowdrifts 7 feet deep on a road rising to 500 feet, with 200 men clearing the way ahead and with 18 horses heaving at the tow lines, whilst men worked uphill towards them from the Bay. The lifeboat was launched two hours after leaving Whitby, and at the second attempt, the crew of the Visitor were saved.

So that future generations may remember the bravery of Coxswain Henry Freeman, and the lifeboatmen, and the dogged determination of the people of Whitby, Hawsker and Robin Hood's Bay, who overcame such difficulties, this memorial was erected in 1981.

Having sampled the delights of the village, we begin the return journey through the fields to Hawsker. There is an excellent view from High Lane looking back across Robin Hood's Bay to Ravenscar. Although the inland path may be less stimulating, there are still some items of interest along the way, including a roadside well as we arrive back at Hawsker. The well, which bears the initials TC and the date 1790, probably supplied water for the whole village until mains water reached the area in the early 1900s.

Start/Parking:	Low Hawsker the Village Hall car park or the adjacent lay-by.
Location:	Low Hawsker is situated on the A171 Whitby to Scarborough road 3 miles (4.8km) south of Whitby.
Grid Ref:	NZ 925 077. – **Postcode:** Mill Lane, Low Hawsker – YO22 4LT.
Distance:	7¾ miles (12.47km) circular. Allow 4½ hrs walking time.
Total Ascent:	1127 feet (343m). – **Maximum Elevation:** 561 feet (171m).
OS Maps:	Explorer OL27 (1:25,000) *North York Moors, Eastern Area* or Landranger 94 (1:50,000) *Whitby and Esk Dale.*
Refreshments:	Robin Hood's Bay and High Hawsker.
Public Toilets:	Robin Hood's Bay.
Other:	Bus service, telephone, Post Office, gift shops, cafes, fish shop, accommodation, information centre.

(1) 925077 From the lay-by or car park entrance turn left and follow the road to the pedestrian crossing.

(2) 925078 Cross the road via the pedestrian crossing and go through a gate to join the Cinder Track *(SP Robin Hood's Bay 3)*. Follow the track to a tarmac lane near the Seaview Caravan Park.

(3) 934078 Turn left and follow the lane to the Northfield Holiday Park.

(4) 939079 Turn left *(SP Robin Hood's Bay 3)* and enter the holiday park. Bear right at a junction and descend along the service road. At the end continue along a grassy track to a sewage works. Bear left and follow the track down to the clifftop.

(5) 941082 Turn right *(SP Cleveland Way - Robin Hood's Bay)* and follow the clifftop path to NT Bay Ness.

(6) 952071 Bear right and descend steeply into the gulley. Cross a couple of footbridges, climb back up and continue to a gate below the coastguard station.

(7) 959064 Pass through the gate, turn left and follow the fence. Go through another gate, turn right, ascend some steps and continue to a gate.

(8) 957059 Go through the gate and follow the left fence. Leave the field via a gate, turn right and pass through two more gates leading to the road at Robin Hood's Bay.

(9) 952055 Follow the road *(Mount Pleasant North)* to the B1447. **CAUTION: Busy road!**

(10) 953049 Turn left and follow the B1447 downhill, keep left at the roundabout and descend to the seafront near the Bay Hotel.

(11) 953049 Return to **point 10**. Turn left into Station Road and continue through the car park passing the former station buildings. Turn right and follow the road for about 50 yards (47m).

(12) 947053 Leave the road via a track on the right *(SP Public Footpath - Madonna House)*. Bear right and turn left at a large shed to follow an enclosed track uphill. Go through a gate and follow the right boundary to the Hook House Farm Campsite. Cross a step stile and follow the gravel road through the site.

(13) 946058 Turn right and follow the road for about 50 yards (47m). Leave the road via a step stile on the left *(SP Public Footpath)*, follow the right boundary uphill. Cross a step stile, bear left slightly and ascend over two more step stiles to High Lane.

(14) 945061 Turn right and follow the road for about ¼ mile (400m). Go through a gate on the left *(SP Public Footpath)*. Follow the left boundary through two fields to Raw Pasture Lane.

(15) 946067 Cross two step stiles and follow the right boundary downhill. Cross a step stile near the right corner and then go through a gate on the left. Follow the left boundary through the field.

(16) 945070 Turn right and follow the farm lane to Bottom House Farm. Pass through the farmyard and go through a gate. Follow the right boundary through three fields.

(17) 938073 Cross a step stile and a wooden bridge, follow the right boundary and go though a gap in the hedge *(Waymark)*. Bear left across the field *(or follow left boundary round)*. Go through a gap in the hedge *(Waymark)* cross the ditch and bear right to cross a step stile hidden in the hedge. Continue directly across the field to the main road. **CAUTION: Busy road!**

(18) 932075 Cross the side road, turn left and follow a path behind the hedge for a short distance *(Sign High Hawsker)*. Cross the road, turn right and follow the road through High Hawsker to the junction with the A171. **CAUTION: Busy road!** .

NB: Although the parking place lies just across the road from the junction, a short diversion to use the pedestrian crossing at **point 2** is recommended. To avoid walking along the main roads completely use **option A**

(A) 932075 Cross the side road and go over a step stile. Follow the left boundary through the field and cross another step stile, returning to the Cinder Track. Turn left and follow the track to the pedestrian crossing at **point 2**. Cross the road, turn left and return to the parking place.

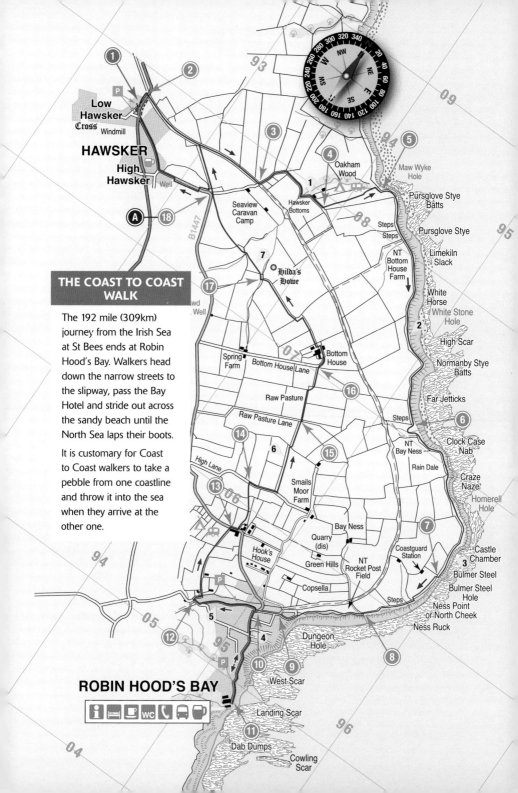

THE COAST TO COAST WALK

The 192 mile (309km) journey from the Irish Sea at St Bees ends at Robin Hood's Bay. Walkers head down the narrow streets to the slipway, pass the Bay Hotel and stride out across the sandy beach until the North Sea laps their boots.

It is customary for Coast to Coast walkers to take a pebble from one coastline and throw it into the sea when they arrive at the other one.

HAWSKER

Low Hawsker
Cross Windmill
High Hawsker
Well

Seaview Caravan Camp

Hawsker Bottoms

Oakham Wood

Maw Wyke Hole

Pursglove Stye Batts

Pursglove Stye

Limekiln Slack

NT Bottom House Farm

White Horse

White Stone Hole

High Scar

Normanby Stye Batts

Far Jetticks

Hilda's Howe

Spring Farm

Bottom House Lane

Bottom House

Raw Pasture

Raw Pasture Lane

Steps

NT Bay Ness

Rain Dale

Clock Case Nab

Craze Naze

Homerell Hole

High Lane

Smails Moor Farm

Bay Ness

Quarry (dis)

Coastguard Station

Castle Chamber

Bulmer Steel

Bulmer Steel Hole

Ness Point or North Cheek

Ness Ruck

Hook's House

Green Hills

NT Rocket Post Field

Copsella

Steps

Dungeon Hole

ROBIN HOOD'S BAY

West Scar

Landing Scar

Dab Dumps

Cowling Scar

Ravenscar and Robin Hood's Bay

FROM RAVENSCAR – 8¾ MILES (14.08KM)

Battlements of the Raven Hall Hotel, Ravenscar

Starting from the windswept heights of Ravenscar, this walk has a diverse variety of impressive scenery to enjoy. The outward path utilises a former railway line which undulates gently to Robin Hood's Bay. Then we follow the graceful curve of the bay, clinging to the coastline for the return to Ravenscar.

In 1895 Victorian entrepreneurs made ambitious plans to turn Ravenscar into a luxurious holiday resort to rival Scarborough and Whitby. The proposals included private houses, hotels, shops, formal gardens, promenade walks and a Marine Esplanade along the cliff top. The company immediately took on 300 workers to construct roads, lay mains drainage and mark out 1500 building plots. In 1900 a brickworks opened, expecting to supply materials for the new town. Unfortunately, few people invested in the project and the company eventually went bankrupt in 1913 after which Ravenscar became famous as 'the town that never was'.

However, the remains of the roads and kerbstones are still visible around the village.

The Raven Hall Hotel, which dates from 1774, was once a private residence owned by King George III's physician, Dr Francis Willis; there is a rumour that the King stayed at the hall for treatment during his bouts of madness. Although the Willis family acquired great wealth, their son Rev. Dr Richard Willis soon squandered his inheritance through an addiction to gambling. According to one story, he lost the hall in a wager which involved two lice crawling across a plate!

Between Ravenscar and Robin Hood's Bay, the route follows the trackbed of the former Scarborough and Whitby Railway line, now known as the 'Cinder Track'. The trail passes the old alum quarry, which was also the site of the Whitaker Brick Company. Despite Ravenscar's demise, the brickworks continued in production, benefitting from having a private railway siding. The company supplied bricks to the expanding town of Scarborough until the 1930s. Demolition of the chimneys took place in the 1960s, but there are substantial remains of the Hoffman kiln.

The track meanders its way round to the former station buildings at Robin Hood's Bay. The waiting rooms and stationmaster's house now provide holiday accommodation, and the station yard serves as the village's main car park. The town has always had a strong connection with the sea, although its thriving fishing fleet began to dwindle in the late nineteenth century and nowadays most of its income derives from tourism.

During the eighteenth century, Robin Hood's Bay was reputedly the busiest smuggling port on the Yorkshire coast. The town's network of tiny streets supposedly has a labyrinth of underground passageways linking the cottages. Therefore contraband could pass from the bay to the top of the village without leaving the cover of the houses. Skirmishes between smugglers and excisemen frequently occurred, both at sea and on land, and smugglers' wives often poured boiling water over the excisemen as they passed through the narrow alleyways. In 1773 two excise cutters, outgunned by three smuggling vessels, had to make a hasty retreat from the bay. Another pitched battle took place in 1779, over 200 kegs of brandy and gin, and fifteen sacks of tea – the smugglers won the day again!

However, the excisemen were not the only threat to bayfolk. In the late eighteenth and early nineteenth centuries, press gangs roamed the coastal villages searching for 'recruits'. Although fishermen were exempt from military service, this did not deter the press gangs; and once 'pressed', the unwilling 'recruits' were unlikely to return home for many years, if at all. The women of the village warned the menfolk by beating a drum when they saw the press gangs arriving; fierce battles followed to beat them off.

Leaving the bay, we follow the clifftop to Ravenscar, dropping down to sea level on just two occasions. The first leads to the beautiful inlet of Boggle Hole, another place associated with legends of hobgoblins. The local name for these mischievous sprites is 'boggle', and they supposedly lived in caves along the coast and the more secluded parts of the moors. Standing to the right of the trail is the youth hostel, which was formerly a water-powered corn mill. Besides accommodation, the hostel has a dog-friendly cafe. The path returns briefly to the clifftop, before crossing the wooded ravine of Stoupe Beck to reach Stoupe Bank Farm.

Further along the clifftop, we pass the remains of a World War II pillbox; one of 28,000 such strongholds constructed c.1940 as part of Britain's defence against the threat of Nazi invasion. The pillbox, which now projects precariously over the edge of the cliff, recently broke into two pieces as a result of coastal erosion. There are glorious views of Robin Hood's Bay, which sweeps in a three-mile curve between the headlands from Ness Point to Old Peak, also known respectively as North Cheek and South Cheek.

Pressing on towards Ravenscar, we pass through the site of the Peak Alum Works, which provides a glimpse into the fascinating industrial past of the area. In the seventeenth century, the discovery of alum in the grey shale around Ravenscar transformed the coastal landscape into an industrialised wasteland. Fifty tons of shale yielded just one ton of alum, and left behind vast quarries and spoil heaps which are still visible on the hillside. The primary uses for alum were as a fixative for dyes and for softening leather during the tanning process. One of the critical ingredients used in its production was human urine! Many natural deodorants contain alum, which prevents the growth of bacteria and eliminates the odour related to sweat; fortunately, these products now utilise synthetic alum.

As we leave the alum works behind, the end of our journey approaches, with the Raven Hall Hotel beckoning behind hilltop battlements. There's also a nine-hole golf course along the way – for those with some energy left!

Start/Parking: Ravenscar has a large car parking bay along the Raven Hall Road. Alternative start from the Station Road car park at Robin Hood's Bay.

Location: Ravenscar is situated off the A171 Whitby to Scarborough road 11 miles (4.8km) north of Scarborough.

Grid Ref: NZ 980 015. – **Postcode:** Raven Hall Road, Ravenscar – YO13 0NA. NZ 947 053. – **Postcode:** Station Road, Robin Hood's Bay – YO22 4RE.

Distance: 8¾ miles (14.08km) circular. Allow 5 hrs walking time.

Total Ascent: 1260 feet (384m). – **Maximum Elevation:** 621 feet (89m).

OS Maps: Explorer OL27 (1:25,000) *North York Moors, Eastern Area* or Landranger 94 (1:50,000) *Whitby and Esk Dale.*

Refreshments: Ravenscar, Boggle Hole YHA and Robin Hood's Bay.

Public Toilets: Ravenscar, Boggle Hole YHA and Robin Hood's Bay.

Other: Telephone, bus service, shops, fish shop.

1 980015 From the parking place walk downhill to the road junction. Turn left and pass the National Trust Visitor Centre. Descend along a concrete road and then follow a path beside a bricked track.

2 977014 Take the left fork *(SP Old Brick Works)* and join the Cinder Track. Follow this almost level track for about 1½ miles (2km) to the arch of a bridge.

3 960025 Pass under the bridge and follow the Cinder Track for a further 1½ miles (2km).

4 945029 Descend some steps and cross the road. Ascend the steps opposite *(SP Cinder Track)* and join a rough driveway, after about 50 yards (48m), bear right and continue along the Cinder Track.

5 947042 Cross the road *(SP Cinder Track to R.H. Bay ¾m)* and pass a caravan site. Go through two gates at Middlewood Farm. Follow the track onto a tarmac lane and continue to the main road.

6 947053 Turn right *(SP Cinder Track)* and follow road for about 20 yards (19m) Turn left *(Sign Village Hall)* and follow a narrow path beside the road. Pass the former station house and enter the car park.

7 950055 Leave the car park, turn left. At the road junction turn right *(SP Cleveland Way - Ravenscar)* and descend along the road into Robin Hood's Bay.

8 953049 Leave Robin Hood's Bay by the side of the Smugglers Bistro *(SP Cleveland Way - Ravenscar 3m - England Coast Path).* Follow the lane to Flagstaff Cottage, ascend some stone steps on the left *(SP Cleveland Way)* and then continue climbing via a wooden boardwalk.

THE BEACH ROUTE

If the tide is receding its possible to walk along the beach to Boggle Hole or Stoupe Beck.

C 953049 Continue down the slipway onto the beach, turn right and proceed along the sands/ rocks to point **D** (12) or point **E** (13).

D E Leave the beach and follow the directions given in point 12 or point 13.

9 952047 Join a stone-paved path and follow it along the top of the cliff.

10 952045 Go through a gate *(SP Cleveland Way - Boggle Hole).* Follow a fenced track and pass through another gate.

11 954041 Descend steeply via some steps into the wooded ravine to the Boggle Hole Youth Hostel and café. Cross Mill Beck via the footbridge and ascend to the road.

12 955040 Turn right and after a few yards leave the road via some steps on the left *(SP Cleveland Way).* Ascend to the clifftop and continue to Stoupe Beck. Descend into the ravine and return to sea level.

13 958035 Cross the bridge *(SP Cleveland Way - Ravenscar)* bear right and follow a stepped path climbing back to the clifftop. Continue to the road at Stoupe Bank Farm. Turn left *(SP Cleveland Way - Ravenscar)* and follow the road for about 300 yards (275m).

14 959031 Leave the road via a stile on the left *(SP Cleveland Way - Ravenscar),* follow an enclosed path through a gate and continue to a World War II pillbox. Now follow the cliff edge passing through a gate and crossing two footbridges. Continue along the track to a signpost.

15 971022 Turn left *(SP Cleveland Way - Alum Works),* cross a footbridge and go through a gate. Continue directly across the field and pass through another gate. Descend into the gully, cross a footbridge and ascend some steps.

16 974021 Leave the alum works at the south side *(Waymark).* Follow an enclosed path to its end. Turn left *(SP Cleveland Way)* and continue on a broad farm track to a fork

17 974018 Take the left fork *(SP Public Footpath)* and ascend through two gates to enter the Raven Hall Golf Course.

18 977016 Follow the track through the course, ascending gradually around a sweeping right bend to the road near the entrance to the Raven Hall Hotel. Turn right and return to the parking place.

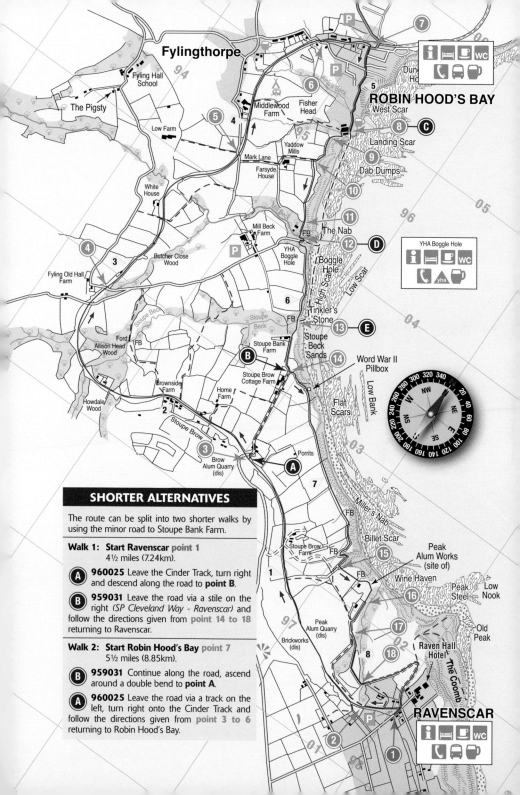

Fylingthorpe

Fyling Hall School

The Pigsty

Low Farm

Fyling Old Hall Farm

White House

Butcher Close Wood

Mill Beck Farm

Middlewood Farm

Fisher Head

Mark Lane

Farsyde House

Yaddow Mills

ROBIN HOOD'S BAY

West Scar

Landing Scar

Dab Dumps

The Nab

YHA Boggle Hole

Boggle Hole

High Scar

Low Scar

Tinkler's Stone

Stoupe Beck Sands

Word War II Pillbox

Flat Scars

Low Bank

Allison Head Wood

Ford
FB

Brownside Farm

Howdale Wood

Home Farm

Stoupe Brow

Stoupe Beck

Stoupe Bank Farm

Stoupe Brow Cottage Farm

Brow Alum Quarry (dis)

Porrits

Miller's Nab

Billet Scar

Stoupe Brow Farm

Peak Alum Works (site of)

Wine Haven

Peak Steel

Low Nook

Old Peak

Peak Alum Quarry (dis)

Brickworks (dis)

Raven Hall Hotel

The Coomb

RAVENSCAR

SHORTER ALTERNATIVES

The route can be split into two shorter walks by
using the minor road to Stoupe Bank Farm.

Walk 1: Start Ravenscar point 1
4½ miles (7.24km)

(A) 960025 Leave the Cinder Track, turn right
and descend along the road to **point B**.

(B) 959031 Leave the road via a stile on the
right (*SP Cleveland Way - Ravenscar*) and
follow the directions given from **point 14 to 18**
returning to Ravenscar.

Walk 2: Start Robin Hood's Bay point 7
5½ miles (8.85km)

(B) 959031 Continue along the road, ascend
around a double bend to **point A**.

(A) 960025 Leave the road via a track on the
left, turn right onto the Cinder Track and
follow the directions given from **point 3 to 6**
returning to Robin Hood's Bay.

Hayburn Wyke and Crook Ness

FROM CLOUGHTON – 7 MILES (11.26KM)

Waterfalls at Hayburn Wyke

The purpose of this walk is to explore the secluded bays between Hayburn Wyke and Crook Ness. Starting from the former Cloughton Station, the route follows another section of the Cinder Track, which provides a link to both ends of this scenic coastal walk.

Although Cloughton is a small village, its facilities are excellent and include a church, pub, tea shop, general store and it also has a regular bus service. St Mary's Church, built in 1831 as a chapel-of-ease, consists of a chancel, nave and a belfry housing three bells. The chancel wall contains a marble plaque in memory of William Bower and his wife Priscilla, dated 1704, which records that William and Priscilla lived long and comfortably in wedlock for 73 years. The inscription includes: 'They live well who love well, They die well who live well'.

The old railway station now functions as a tea room, which has an impressive selection of snacks, delicious cakes and scones to

enjoy; and a guest house with en-suite bed and breakfast rooms. There is also a well-refurbished railway carriage named 'Oscar', sitting on the former track for those who prefer self-catering.

From Cloughton, we head north along the Cinder Track to Hayburn Wyke. Although the trackbed is relatively level and easy to follow, cyclists and horse-riders also use the track, so look back occasionally. In addition to its recreational value, the Cinder Track also serves as a wildlife corridor, which enables species to move safely between the varied habitats along its length. Bats and owls exploit the cutting during the twilight hours, along with other nocturnal creatures such as badgers, foxes and hedgehogs.

The Hayburn Wyke Hotel is a traditional eighteenth-century coaching inn and was reputedly an old smugglers' haunt. However, the shoreline in the bay below would have made it difficult to beach boats without risking substantial damage to the vessels. Carrying contraband across the rocky beach would be equally hazardous, especially if caught unawares by the excisemen.

After partaking of refreshments at the inn, we descend to the secluded cove of Hayburn Wyke where twin waterfalls cascade directly onto the boulder-strewn beach. The name is a combination of 'Hayburn', an Anglo-Saxon word meaning 'hunting enclosure by a stream' and 'Wyke' from the Norse word 'Vik' which means 'sea inlet' or 'creek'.

The densely wooded slopes are a haven for wildlife, with more than thirty species of breeding birds recorded, including blackcaps, spotted flycatchers, redstarts, willow warblers and woodpeckers. Badgers, foxes and roe deer frequent the forest fringes, while smaller mammals take refuge in the understorey. In spring and early summer, wildflowers embellish the woodland with one spectacular display after another. Clusters of wood anemone mingle in the yellow swathes of celandine, and then wild garlic compliments a carpet of bluebells, followed by other ground flora including lady's mantle and wild honeysuckle.

Meanwhile, on the rocky shore, marine life flourishes in shallow rock pools, after being stranded by the receding tide. The plants and small creatures that live in these intertidal habitats have all evolved to help them survive the harsh conditions of the coastal environment. Blennies and butterfish share their short-term home with anemones, barnacles, dog whelks, limpets, periwinkles and the odd crab, waiting for the returning tides to replenish their pools and submerge them back into deep water.

Leaving the beach, we join the Cleveland Way long-distance trail which ascends through the wood to Little Cliff. During the summer, the clifftop hedgerow yields a succession of ripening berries, including blackberry, elderberry, rose hips and sloes – providing a feast for both wildlife and foragers!

Just after gaining the summit at Roger Trod, Scarborough Castle appears on the distant headland, and although it's some six miles away, the castle dominates the distant skyline as we progress along the coastal path. Clinging to the coastline, we cross a small ravine at Salt Pans; the name refers to the large rocks on the shore where fisherfolk once evaporated seawater to produce salt. Before the advent of refrigeration, salt was a vital commodity in fishing communities for the preservation of the catch.

A little further on, we pass around the beautiful cove of Cloughton Wyke, a shingle inlet enclosed by high cliffs, very popular with sea anglers. Across the bay, the cliffs at Hundale Point provide excellent nesting for seabird colonies. From the Point, we sweep around the headland, passing the old coastguard lookout station at Long Nab to reach Crook Ness.

The lookout station dates from 1927 with a mine shelter added in 1939 to protect the coastguards during World War II. One of its primary functions was to look for mines or torpedoes which signified the presence of enemy submarines operating near the Scarborough Channel sea lane; this was of considerable importance to the safety of all UK and allied shipping. In 1945 the station reverted to its pre-war role. However, the station played a part in the Carrier Control Nuclear Warning System until the early 1960s. The station closed in 1993 and Scarborough Birders now use it for bird watching and the study of migration.

At Crook Ness, a ravine leads down to the beach and provides another opportunity to explore this magnificent coastline at close quarters. During the Victorian era, the gorge provided access to the shoreline for the collection of rocks and stones used for road building. There is evidence of donkeys being used for this purpose, carrying panniers laden with stone.

Leaving the coastline behind the final leg returns inland to the Cinder Track, which leads us back to Cloughton Station. Moreover, if the tea room is still open, you may wish to indulge in some of those sumptuous treats mentioned earlier!

Start/Parking: Car park at the Station House Tearooms, Cloughton YO13 0AD.

Alternative parking is available in several places including a sizeable car park at the end of Field Lane near Crook Ness.

Location: Cloughton is situated off the A171 Scarborough to Whitby road 4.5 miles (7.24km) north of Scarborough.

Grid Ref: TA 011 940. – **Postcode:** Station Lane, Cloughton, YO13 0AD.

Distance: 7 miles (11.26km) circular. Allow 4 hrs walking time.

Total Ascent: 843 feet (257m). – **Maximum Elevation:** 363 feet (111m).

OS Maps: Explorer OL27 (1:25,000) *North York Moors, Eastern Area* or Landranger 101 (1:50,000) *Scarborough.*

Refreshments: Cloughton and Hayburn Wyke.

Public Toilets: None en route.

Other: Bus service, telephone, Post Office, gift shops, cafes.

1 **011940** From the car park entrance turn right and follow the road for about 10 yards (9m). Leave the road via a gate on the left *(SP Whitby 17m),* and join the Cinder Track, part of the National Cycle Network.

2 **013948** Pass under the bridge *(entering the National Park),* and follow the track for about 1½ miles (2.4km) to the road near the Hayburn Wyke Inn.

3 **007968** Turn right and follow the road to the Hayburn Wyke Inn. After passing the inn go through a gate. Bear right and descend along a grassy track towards the woodland.

4 **007970** Go through a gate and descend onto a broad track. Continue downhill on a clear path which leads to the twin waterfalls at Hayburn Wyke.

5 **010971** After visiting the falls return to the footbridge, bear left and ascend the stone-paved path. Turn left *(SP Cleveland Way - Scarborough 5½m)* and follow the waymarks and signposts ascending through the wood.

6 **009968** Turn left *(SP Cleveland Way - Scarborough 5½m),* and ascend from the wood, now follow the clifftop to a bench seat. *(A memorial to Ann M Hazell, the President of Scarborough Rambling Club from 1978-1993).*

7 **017961** Bear left and follow the clifftop path *(SP Cleveland Way)* to a wooded ravine.

8 **020957** Descend steeply and cross the ravine. Continue along the cliff path and cross over the small ravine at Salt Pans.

9 **020952** Bear left *(SP Cleveland Way - Scarborough 4 miles)* and ascend some steps. Continue along the clifftop path which leads to Cloughton Wyke.

10 **020950** At a three-way marker post bear left and descend to cross Cloughton Wyke. Climb some steps leading back to the clifftop. Continue across two more ravines to reach the Long Nab Coastguard Station. *(Leaving the National Park).*

11 **029940** From the coastguard station continue along the clifftop path to Crook Ness.

12 **026936** At a waymark post, leave the Cleveland Way and continue onto a tarmac lane. Follow the lane for about ¾ mile (1.2km) to reach the former railway bridge.

13 **016931** After passing under the bridge, leave the road and ascend some steps on the left which lead back onto the Cinder Track. Turn left and follow the track which returns to the parking place and the Station House Tearooms.

ALTERNATIVE ROUTES

The route can be split into two shorter walks by using Salt Pan Road to link the two halves. The first option below shortens the main route by approximately 2 miles (3.2km).

A **020952** Turn right *(SP Cloughton ¾ mile)* and ascend to the Salt Pan Road. Follow the road over a bridge crossing the Cinder Track.

B **013948** Immediately after crossing the bridge, turn right and descend some steps. Turn right, pass under the bridge and follow the Cinder Track back to the road at Cloughton. Turn right and return to the car park.

To undertake the second half of the route, leave the Cinder Track at **point 2 (B)** and follow the Salt Pan Road to **point 9 (A)**. Turn right and then continue using the directions given from **point 9**.

HAYBURN WYKE BEACH

The beach is strewn with large rocks and boulders, which makes it difficult to walk around on, especially when wet. Therefore it's advisable to wear boots with sufficient ankle support.

Red House Farm

FB

FB

Hayburn Wyke Inn

Hayburn Wyke (Nature Reserve)

97

Little Cliff

Tindall Point

Newlands Dale

3

Iron Scar

Cloughton Woods

Cloughton Newlands Farm

Roger Trod

02

03

Cloughton Newlands

96

Greystone Farm

Little Moor

Sycarham Farm

Cober

4

Salt Pans

A

Cloughton Wyke

Salt Pan Road

95

Court Green Farm

Hundale Scar

Goose Dale

A171

Cloughton

Hun Dale

Hundale Point

Quarry Banks

Cloughton Fields Farm

The Hundales

Cloughton Quarries (disused)

94

5

Creek Point

Long Nab

Long Nab Coastguard Station

Burniston

National Park Boundary

Cliff Top House

6

Field Lane

Crook Ness

Flat Scar

93

A171

A165

Miscellanea

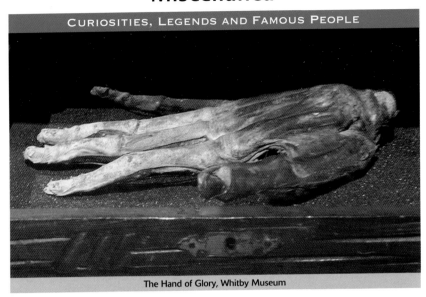

The Hand of Glory, Whitby Museum

The North Yorkshire and Cleveland Heritage Coast has a fascinating history with a wealth of intriguing stories and wonderful customs. Here are just a few of the interesting tales and famous people associated with the area.

THE HAND OF GLORY

In the early twentieth century, Joseph Ford, a stonemason and local historian discovered a mummified human hand hidden inside the wall of a cottage in Castleton. He instantly recognised it from well-known legends of such artefacts as a 'Hand of Glory'. Since 1935, the Hand has been an exhibit at Whitby Museum, and it is the only known 'Hand of Glory' still in existence.

A Hand of Glory was supposedly the pickled right hand of a hanged felon, severed from the body while it was still hanging from the gallows; a prized possession used by burglars. According to one version of the story, the burglar would enter a dwelling and light a candle made from human fat clenched by the hand. Allegedly this action had the power to send sleepers in the house into a deep coma from which they were unable to awake. However, in the Whitby version, the outstretched hand has its own fingers lit. In this case, if one of the fingers refused to light it was a sign that someone in the household was still awake. It was not possible to extinguish the light by water or pinching, but only by blood or skimmed milk.

The burglar supposedly chanted the following verse as he lit the Hand of Glory:

Let those who rest more deeply sleep,

Let those awake their vigils keep,

O, Hand of Glory, shed thy light,

Guide us to our spoils tonight.

Once lit, the hand provided illumination for the holder, while others remained in darkness. Some accounts say that the hand made the holder invisible and also gave them the power to unlock any door which they came across.

The term 'hand of glory' possibly derived from 'main de gloire', which is a corruption of 'mandragore', the French word for mandrake. The root has hallucinogenic and narcotic properties, and in sufficient quantities, it induces a state of unconsciousness. The belief that the mandrake's leaves glow at night led to one of its names in Arabic, meaning 'Devils candle', which may have added to the idea of a lamp for criminals.

Sir Walter Scott recounts the alleged powers of the hand in his 1816 gothic novel *The Antiquary*, and he also describes its macabre preparation. The story of the hand has also featured in several films over the years. In the 1973 film *The Wicker Man*, the innkeeper tries to put Sergeant Howie to sleep using a Hand of Glory. The light has such power that the innkeeper's daughter expresses concern that 'he might sleep for days.' In the 2002 film *Harry Potter and the Chamber of Secrets*, a Hand of Glory appears when Harry finds himself in Knockturn Alley.

THE SUNKEN BELLS OF WHITBY ABBEY

During the reign of Henry VIII, Whitby Abbey and many other religious buildings fell victim to the Dissolution of the Monasteries, with all their valuables confiscated to generate income for the Crown. However, the King wanted to keep the abbey's ring of bells, described as 'very noble and antique'. The King instructed his commissioners to remove the bells, carry them down the 199 steps and load them onto a waiting ship for transport to London. Although devastated by the actions of the king, the townspeople could do nothing to prevent their beloved chimes being taken away. A crowd gathered and watched in tears as the ship left the harbour. Some people prayed that something would happen to keep the bells in Whitby, far away from London.

Subsequently and without warning, shortly after setting sail from the harbour the ship capsized and sank just offshore near Black Nab. Even though it was probably the extreme weight of the bells which caused the boat to founder, some versions of the story suggest that it was divine intervention, to prevent the blatant theft of church property.

According to sailors and local fishermen, the sunken bells can still be heard tolling beneath the waves, especially in stormy seas.

THE MERMAIDS OF STAITHES

Before Staithes became a busy fishing town with a small population, two beautiful mermaids were caught out in a terrible storm, washed up on the beach and fell asleep from exhaustion. When they awoke, they found themselves held captive in fishing nets with the villagers gazing in amazement. Although the mermaids pleaded for their freedom, explaining that they meant no harm and had just been trying to find shelter from the dreadful storm, no one listened.

Eventually, the villagers realised that the mermaids were friendly and began providing them with food and gifts. After many months of imprisonment, the mermaids managed to charm one of the fishermen, and he agreed to let them out of the nets for a moment. The mermaids seized this opportunity and made their escape to the safety of the sea before the villagers realised what was happening.

One of the mermaids turned around and looked back at the place which had held her captive. Rising up on her fluttering tail, she shouted out in anger and put a curse on the town crying 'The sea shall flow to Jackdaw's Well.' The villagers scoffed at the curse, as Jackdaw's Well was a long way inland in those days. The well derived its name from the flocks of jackdaws which assembled there.

Nevertheless, the mermaid's curse did come true. Over the years, coastal erosion has caused many cottages and fields to collapse into the sea, and Jackdaw's Well disappeared long ago.

Mermaid lintel, Staithes

JEANIE BIGGERSDALE OF MULGRAVE WOODS

The sylvan expanse of Mulgrave Woods is a peaceful place in which to wander. However, take care not to disturb the solitude of Jeanie Biggersdale – a very ill-tempered fairy with a strong dislike for visitors. Anyone interrupting her tranquillity faces a terrible curse and the risk of being killed!

One story tells of a drunken farmer from Eskdale, who accepted a wager to visit Jeanie and confront her. The farmer jumped on his horse and made his way to the evil sprite's cave. Still fortified by alcohol, he began calling for Jeanie to come out and reveal herself. Unfortunately, for him, Jeanie was at home and abruptly responded that she was coming.

The anger in her voice struck terror into the farmer, and he turned his horse to flee, but Jeanie was in hot pursuit. Fortunately, he remembered that witches and fairies cannot cross running water and made his escape by jumping over a stream. However, Jeanie had managed to touch the rear flanks of the farmer's horse before it was entirely across, which resulted in the poor animal being cut in half. Having survived his ordeal, the farmer returned home, horseless and completely sober; and never bothered Jeanie again!

So, if you do go for a walk in Mulgrave Woods, make sure you don't anger this resident fairy.

WADE'S STONE

Standing in a field to the north of the tiny hamlet of East Barnby is the Wade's Stone, supposedly named after a legendary giant who lived in a castle near Lythe. When Henry VIII's topographer, John Leland, passed through here c.1535, he records that there were two stones standing 11 feet (3.4m) apart called Wadda's Grave. Another stone near Goldsborough bears the same name, and this also formerly had a second stone, set 100 feet (30m) apart. In local folklore, the distance between the original pairs of stones represented the head and foot of Wade's enormous grave. Therefore, he may have been 100 feet tall – large enough to take on King Kong!

Although, in reality, both the remaining monoliths date back to the Neolithic or early Bronze Age and could be well over 5000 years old. The stones may have been markers to indicate tribal boundaries, ancient pathways or meeting places. In 2008 the East Barnby stone toppled over, possibly due to centuries of cultivation around its base. The North York Moors National Park Authority appointed Tees Archaeology to reinstate the fallen stone. After careful excavation, they extended the depth of the original socket hole to provide an adequate trench in which to set the re-erected stone.

Wade's Stone, East Barnby

According to one legend, Wade, together with his wife, Bell, built castles at Mulgrave and Pickering. Each of them constructing one castle, and apparently, they only had one hammer, which they tossed back and forth across the moor, a distance of 17 miles! In due course, the couple settled down and kept cattle on the moors. To make it easier for his wife to reach the cows and bring them in for milking, Wade built a road across the moor – now known as Wade's Causeway.

THE REPUS

The *Repus* is a traditional fishing coble that was found in bad repair at the South Gare, near the mouth of the River Tees. After bringing the boat back to the Grove, records revealed that she had once belonged to a Skinningrove fisherman who died in the 1980s. The *Repus* first put to sea at Redcar in 1963 and retired from the fishing register in November 1996. In 2008 the local community decided to restore the *Repus*, and they added two carved figures; she now provides a fitting memorial to all those lost at sea off the Grove.

Nearby stands the kedge anchor from the SS *Sylvania*, which ran aground on Cattersty Sands in 1901, where it remained stranded for six months. The anchor's salvage took place in 2001, after being buried in the sands for 100 years.

The Repus, Skinningrove

THE PENNY HEDGE

Traditionally, the Penny Hedge ceremony began in 1159, when the Abbot of Whitby imposed a penance on three noblemen, and their descendants for all time, after they murdered a hermit at Eskdale.

The nobles were hunting a wild boar which took refuge in a hermitage. The monk living there shut out the chasing hounds and set about helping the wounded animal. The hunting party burst into the chapel, raging at the monk's interference and struck him down with their spears. After dragging himself from the chapel to get help, he was rushed to Whitby Abbey, but his wounds were too severe. Before he died, the monk told the abbot that he would forgive the hunters, thus sparing their lives, if they agreed to carry out a penance.

Consequently, the abbot confiscated the noblemen's lands as punishment, but he agreed that they could lease them back as long as they and their descendants performed an annual penance – the Penny Hedge.

Each year on the eve of Ascension Day, which falls forty days after Easter Sunday,

the men had to construct a short hedge in the harbour. The hedge had to be strong enough to withstand three tides and built from hawthorn cut down with a knife costing just one penny. Moreover, if the hedge failed, they would forfeit their lands to Whitby Abbey.

The date chosen for this task assured that there would be a low tide, but 'if the sea should ever be too high to finish the hedge by 9 am, then the penance would be discharged'. In 1981 after more than 800 years, a 'full sea' did prevent the construction of the hedge, thus fulfilling this clause. Nevertheless, the tradition of the Penny Hedge continues, and if you visit Whitby on Ascension Eve, you can watch the hedge being built in the upper harbour.

According to historians, the Penny Hedge is a relic of a feudal ritual known as Horngarth, which dates back to the twelfth century. This required tenants to maintain the fences and hedges that divided their lands. If tenants failed to perform this task, the landowner had the right to evict them, or he could impose a public penance, such as building a fence in the harbour.

CAPTAIN JAMES COOK

James Cook, the British navigator and explorer, rose from humble beginnings to become the most legendary seaman of his time. Moreover, he discovered and accurately charted the entire coastline of New Zealand and the Great Barrier Reef of Australia.

Born on 27 October 1728, at Marton-in-Cleveland, Yorkshire, James Cook was the son of a Scottish farm worker and grew up on a farm near Great Ayton, where he attended the village school. In 1744 James moved to Staithes as an apprentice in the shop of William Sanderson. However, It was not long before 16-year-old James became fascinated by seafaring tales and dreamed of becoming a seaman. In July 1746 Cook began a three-year apprenticeship in the Merchant Navy with Captain John Walker, a Quaker coal-shipper from Whitby, and his proficiency in mathematics and navigation emerged.

Although Captain Walker offered him a command in 1755, Cook decided to join the Royal Navy instead, and within a month he was master's mate aboard HMS *Eagle*. Two years later, he became the master of HMS *Pembroke*, which played a significant role in charting the approaches to Quebec up the St. Lawrence River in Canada and led to the capture of Louisburg and Quebec.

James Cook's first voyage as an explorer began in 1768 when he left England in command of HM *Bark Endeavour*. Although his mission was to observe the transit of Venus across the face of the sun from Tahiti, he also had sealed orders instructing him to find the 'Great Southern Continent' for which he found no evidence. Nevertheless, his search led to the discovery of New Zealand and Australia.

During his second voyage in 1772-75 Cook's ships crossed the Antarctic circle numerous times, but the intense cold forced them to turn back. However, he dispelled the myth of an undiscovered southern continent, and on his return to England, he became the first person to circumnavigate the world in both directions.

Captain Cook statue, Whitby

On his third and final voyage in 1776-79 Cook's primary objective was to search for the existence of an entrance to the North West Passage which linked the Atlantic and Pacific oceans. In January 1778 he discovered the Hawaiian Islands, naming them the Sandwich Islands after his patron the Earl of Sandwich.

During his first visit to Hawaii, Cook received a warm welcome; the natives treated him and his crew with great respect, providing them with gifts and food. In February 1778 Cook sailed from Hawaii to the North American coast heading to Alaska in search of the North West Passage. Evidently, Cook came to within 50 miles (80km) of the entrance, but thick ice floes and violent currents in the Bering Sea prevented him from locating it. The expedition sailed back to the warmer waters of the Hawaiian Islands, arriving there in December 1778 to prepare for another attempt the following season.

After making a circumnavigation of Hawaii, which took over a month, the ships dropped anchor in Kealakekua Bay on 16 January 1779. Over 1000 canoes came out to greet them; apparently, Cook's arrival had coincided with celebrations marking the Hawaiian religious festival of Makahiki to their fertility god – Lono. The Hawaiians seemingly treated Cook and his crew as gods during this second visit, until one of the crewmen died, revealing that they were just mere mortals and relationships became agitated. The expedition left the islands on 4 February 1779. However, high gales broke the foremast of HMS *Resolution*, forcing Cook to return to Kealakekua Bay to make repairs. On this occasion, the natives were less friendly, and they stole the cutter of HMS *Discovery*. The following day, the 14 February 1779, Cook put ashore with nine marines to demand the cutter's return. Without warning, warriors attacked the shore party with clubs, spears and knives killing Cook and four of the marines.

The natives removed Cook's body from the beach, and after preserving his hands in sea salt, they cut his body into pieces and stripped the flesh from the bones; the Hawaiian custom in the treatment of the remains of a high chief. According to tradition the owner of such bones inherited the spiritual power of the deceased. When peace resumed, the Hawaiians returned parts of Cook's body which included his skull and hands. The remains were placed in a casket and consigned to the waters of Kealakekua Bay on 21 February 1779.

HM *BARK ENDEAVOUR*

Captain Cook's most famous ship was the *Endeavour*, which he used on his first voyage. Previously called the *Earl of Pembroke*, the vessel was a Whitby cat, or collier, designed to transport coal from the north-east of England to London. After being refitted for the voyage, the Admiralty renamed and commissioned her as HM *Bark Endeavour*. The name 'Bark' identified her from another *Endeavour*, already in service at the time. The ship accommodated nearly one hundred officers and crew, marines and civilians, and it was the crew's main home during the three-year voyage. A full-scale replica of HM *Bark Endeavour*, now forms part of a tourist attraction in Endeavour Wharf.

FRANK MEADOW SUTCLIFFE

Frank Meadow Sutcliffe

Frank Meadow Sutcliffe, born in 1853 at Headingley in Leeds, was a pioneer of photography as an art form; his studies of Victorian Whitby capture the life and tradition of that period intimately. From the mid-1870s until his death in 1941, Sutcliffe worked in Whitby. After retiring from photography in 1922, he became the curator of the Whitby Literary and Philosophical Society Museum.

Although portraiture provided his primary income and won him numerous medals at international exhibitions, Sutcliffe is most famous for his landscape and documentary photographs. These incorporate everyday working people in Whitby and the beautiful surrounding countryside, the harbour, fishing and fisher-folk – each one carefully posed. Most of these were taken for his own satisfaction, and Sutcliffe's affection and respect for Whitby and the local people are evident in his compositions.

One of Sutcliffe's most famous photographs is the 'Water Rats', which shows a group of naked boys playing around a boat. However, the print landed him in considerable trouble, after the local clergy cited it as a work 'to the corruption of the young of the other sex', and then excommunicated him!

SALTBURN TRAMWAY AND PIER

Saltburn has one of the world's oldest water balanced inclined tramways. Its two cars, each fitted with a large water tank beneath, travel on parallel tracks. The weight of the top car is increased by adding water to its tank until it outweighs that of the lower car. At this point, gravity takes over allowing the top car to descend to the bottom, and the process begins all over again by recycling the water to the top. A brakeman controls the entire operation from his cabin at the top of the incline. The tramway links the town with its splendid pleasure pier; the last surviving iron pier on England's north-east coastline.

When the pier opened in May 1869, it was 1500 feet (457m) long and had a landing stage for paddle-steamers. During the first six months, more than fifty thousand people

Saltburn's Tramway and Pier

paid to stroll along it. Unfortunately, in October 1875 a storm destroyed the pier-head landing stage and a section of the deck, reducing its length to 1250 feet (381m). Throughout its long history, the pier has had to close several times for repairs due to storm damage. In May 1924 the SS *Ovenbeg* crashed into the structure causing a 210-foot (64m) gap, subsequently repaired. But the most significant threat came in 1975 when the council applied for a demolition order. However, a 'Save the Pier' campaign led to a public inquiry which decided that only the last thirteen piles should be removed, reducing the pier's length to 681 feet (208m). The pier is still a major attraction for visitors, and in 2009 the National Piers Society voted it 'Pier of the Year'.

A GREEK TEMPLE FOR PIGS

In the late nineteenth century Squire John Warren Barry of Fyling Hall, near Robin Hood's Bay, built a mock Greek temple to serve as a pigsty for two of his beloved sows. The squire was somewhat eccentric and obviously thought that his pigs were worth pampering in this way. Evidently, he loathed the Victorian practice of pigsties in the backyards of cottages.

Apparently, Squire Barry had a passionate interest in the architecture of the Etruscan and Greek buildings on the island of Corsica, which most likely inspired his design. The craftsmanship is remarkable; the facade consists of a pediment surmounting a columned porch, elaborately decorated in ochre, gold and red.

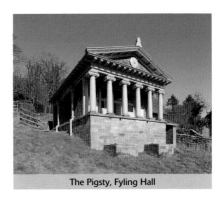

The Pigsty, Fyling Hall

Whether the pigs enjoyed the lavish conditions imposed on them is uncertain, but the pigsty, after suitable refurbishment, is now available to holiday-makers. The building was the model for its namesake as one of Lilliput Lane's collectable miniature cottages.